New Edge of the Anvil

New Edge of the Anvil

A Resource Book
for the Blacksmith

Written and Illustrated by
Jack Andrews

SkipJack Press, Inc.
Ocean Pines, MD

Library of Congress Cataloging in Publication Data

Andrews, Jack
    New Edge of the Anvil

    Bibliography:p.
    Includes index.
    1. Blacksmithing.   I. Title
Library of Congress Catalog Card Number
    94-92314

ISBN 1-879535-09-2

Printed in the United States of America

2 4 6 8 10 9 7 5 3

Also by Jack Andrews
Samuel Yellin, Metalworker

Contents

Contents

Contents

Contents

List of Charts

Preface

The intent of the *Edge of the Anvil*, when it was first published in 1977, was to provide the information to set up a forge, the knowledge of tools and forging process enabling you to teach yourself blacksmithing. This idea has not changed with the *New Edge of the Anvil*. But, what I have done is added resource information, corrections, eliminated outdated information, added more exercises and changes in the type of exercises. Emphasis has been put on design, the use of the computer and modern tools. The reasons are some information has changed, new knowledge has been realized and the nature of the village blacksmith has changed to that of the contemporary metalworker. I intend the *New Edge* to be a reflection of this new artist/blacksmith.

Even though this image has changed, I still emphasize the importance of examining beautiful old tools and pieces of wrought iron, deciphering the processes that were used to make them. It is by understanding the techniques that were used by our grandfathers that we can again be workers of iron. Unfortunately, many of the smiths who made these pieces have laid down their hammers, and the techniques have not been passed on to others. By examining these pieces closely, we can see how these masters worked and can get a glimpse of the processes that they used to create more complex pieces. This is the reason I have included the photographs of Samuel Yellin's work. Yellin may have seen what was happening to wrought iron years ago when he said, "The cause for the lack of development of iron craft in this country is that iron is used as a barrier and not as a bridge." The barrier that Yellin was referring to was a barrier created by the need for security. The bridge was a visual bridge—to view out into the world. The Yellin portfolio was originally intended to serve as a guide to how small pieces and fragments were made. To better explain how a Yellin piece is made, Fred Crist now shows a technique he rediscovered. This section is called "Edges of the Anvil."

To add to the work from the past, another portfolio has also been added: the work of Martin Rose, a metalworker and contemporary of Yellin, whose work encompassed the Art Deco style.

I have also included demonstrations of work by contemporary smiths to show the type of iron that is being created today. I would emphasize that by examining the work of today's smiths much can also be learned. A bridge is shown by several contemporary smiths, selected to demonstrate a varied and different view of their work along with the exercises that explain the work. Certainly not acting as a barrier but as a bridge to view our contemporary world.

It is to this sense of rediscovery, creativity and the new generation of blacksmiths that I dedicate this book.

If you have any thoughts or comments please write to me at, SkipJack Press Inc., 6 Laport Court, 1408-B Ocean Pines, MD, 21811; or contact me via e-mail <skipjack@shore.intercom.net>. To order books call 1-800-247-6553.

Jack Andrews
Ocean Pines, 1997

New Edge of the Anvil

New Focus on Blacksmithing

My grandfather, like many blacksmiths of yesteryear, brings to mind an image of robust and independent craftsmen who were a main force in the early history of our country. They were central figures in the life of the villages, because they provided most of the tools and implements that were needed for the life of the community. The scale of work was small, personal and communal. These men were also forceful in the development of new industrial processes and the invention of tools and products. They widened the range of goods and products that this newly created force brought about. They were part of the industrial revolution and helped spur it on.

Craftsmen changed their methods and scale of working from one-of-a-kind to production of many. These changes, along with advances in technology, brought about their own demise: the disappearance of the individual craftsman. The result was a change from the small shop run, by the individual, multipurpose craftsman to the large factory, hiring specialized workers for mass-production. The small-scale operation of the blacksmith was consequently lost to an abundance of mass-produced goods. This was the experience of my grandfather and the business that he created.

Too frequently, we have criticized mass-production without seeing any of its benefits. One benefit is that, with an abundance of goods, today's craftsmen have been freed to produce those things that have individuality and character. There have been several generations since the industrial revolution, and we now have the opportunity to reexamine the manner in which we choose to work and live.

During the last decade, blacksmithing has grown, not only in the number of working smiths, but also in the greatly varying types of iron work being done: architecture, jewelry, sculpture and an abundance of utilitarian products. There are many people who have changed careers, bringing a rich dynamic of new ideas and thoughts into the metalworking areas. Blacksmithing used to be a male-dominated activity; now there are many full-time smiths and metalworkers who are female. The state of blacksmithing is changing it's focus.

Perhaps your work with blacksmithing will allow you to reorder your priorities, giving emphasis to new values and providing a new focus on your lifestyle based upon your own individuality and character.

Graham Scott Williamson, in his book, *The American Craftsman*, questions:

Where does craft production stop and industrial production begin? . . . Our conception of craft as consisting of the spirit in which, rather than solely the means by which a production process is carried out. This would appear to be the only conception of craft and craftsmanship which can hope to take root in this technologically advanced age.

Later he quotes Allen Eaton of the Russell Sage Foundation:

"The time will come when every kind of work will be judged by two measurements: one by the product itself, as is now done, and the other by the effect of the work on the producer. I believe this leads us to some realization that there is hope for the future and that we do not have to be puppets of our culture and technology, but can be forceful in redirecting the thought and movement of our society, if we, as individual craftsmen, set an example by means of our attitudes to our work and towards others."

The ideas set forth and the alternatives suggested in E. F. Schumacher's book, *Small Is Beautiful*, are in striking contrast to the general direction of our country today. Those who read the book may come to feel, as I do, that new attitudes and priorities may be in order.

At a time when there is so much emphasis placed on progress, growth and expansion on a worldwide scale, it is almost heresy to say, "small is beautiful." But the two elements can coexist. It is precisely because of the fast pace of all of our lives, the huge industries, vast population and overwhelming bureaucracy, that a reexamination of our values is essential. We see this all around us in the resurgence of interest in crafts of all kinds, in such small things as vegetable gardens and in a return to the simpler life. I feel that the village blacksmith's smaller scale of work is a paradigm with which we can temper today's living. We need not ignore the advances of science and technology, but we must recognize that in the haste to acquire and consume, we ourselves will be consumed.

The world is too much with us, late and soon.
Getting and spending, we lay waste our powers.... [W. Wordsworth]

Gandhi proposed that we think in terms of "production by the masses" rather than in terms of "mass production." The small scale smithy or studio, where only one or two people work, would certainly fall into this category. If work by its nature ennobles and enlightens, then we are working on the development of mind, body and spirit. A technology of production by the masses would use the best of modern knowledge and experience to help us live in ecological balance in the world. It would serve the people in contrast to a world devoted to mass production where the people serve the machine. Schumacher calls this Gandhian philosophy "intermediate technology."

I believe that some contemporary blacksmiths have a focus that represents intermediate technology. Others use the advances of modern technology, which includes the use of laser cutting technology and the computer, but still maintain the scale of the individual craftsman. These artists/craftspersons still take pride in each object that they make and derive pleasure from the creation of beautiful forms, tools and utensils.

The poetry of the blacksmith shop has been a theme for writers for centuries, but there is little poetry in it to the blacksmith who stands at the forge day after day pounding and shaping unless he has studied, and finds new themes in every heat, spark or scale. If he can create beautiful forms in his mind and with his hands shape the metal to those forms then he can see poetry in his work. If he is but a machine that performs his work automatically, the dull prose of his occupation makes him dissatisfied and unmanly.   [M. T. Richardson; *Practical Blacksmithing*, vol. III]

Many smiths and metalworkers today are very definitely poets of iron! How do you see your forging, as poetry or work? To me, that poetic realness is more important than quantity and sameness, especially if one wishes—as I do—to realize satisfaction.

The Workshop

Your first look around a metalworker's studio might be confusing because of the great variety of unfamiliar tools and equipment covered with dust, seemingly in disarray and poor light. However, an experienced smith looks in on an order and working arrangement with the light of knowledge. This chapter is organized to bring that order and light as you begin your study of black-smithing.

The Smithy

The smithy is the building in which the blacksmith works. This term is frequently confused with another, the smith, which is the person doing the blacksmithing. Don't, however, confuse the space in which the smith works with the way he feels about it. Proper working relationships and attitudes must exist for good work to be done.

My first smithy was a shed with one side open. It was a starting point, but I allowed junk to clutter the working space, and soon things were disorganized. I soon realized that this had an adverse effect on the way I worked. I was easily frustrated. I began to plan and think about the different types of buildings I could construct. After a long search, I discovered what I was looking for: the tipi. I ordered the canvas cover from California and cut the poles in the wood behind my house. The tipi is 20 feet in diameter. The sun filtered through the canvas, providing good working light all day. By adjusting the smoke flaps, I could control the ventilation. On stormy days when there was a strong

Smoke flaps open on the tipi.

southerly wind, I did not work; I watched the woods instead. The tipi was not expensive, was easy to erect and was portable. The township where I lived did not allow permanent buildings or industrial buildings, and my tipi avoided these restrictions.

The tipi had another quality which was important to me (aside from being true American Architecture): the quality of the workspace. It was a truly enjoyable place to work and I liked being there. The tipi was quiet when forging (sounds did not reverberate) and then there were only the sounds of the woods when not forging.

I worked in the tipi for five years. Because I was forging larger work, I needed more room and had to expand. My next smithy was an old brick building, 60x60 with a 25-foot ceiling. There was ample room to do many different things and to acquire a wide range of tools—along with an excess of junk. After considerable experimentation in setting up the shop I went back to the process that I used in the tipi and simplified the layout.

I have concluded that there is no ideal smithy. Plan one to suit yourself, using available space, but keeping in mind the efficiency of a simple layout.

The primary consideration when building or organizing the smithy should be adequate space. Set aside an area as you begin to collect your equipment and try different arrangements. (You can work outside, but this should only be a temporary arrangement.) Now consider the ways in which various pieces of equipment interact. Things may be convenient and orderly, but unless they relate in a functional manner, it will be more difficult to work.

Working Relationships

The diagrams of the tipi floor plan show the relationships of the pieces of equipment. They are drawn to scale relative to the amount of time spent

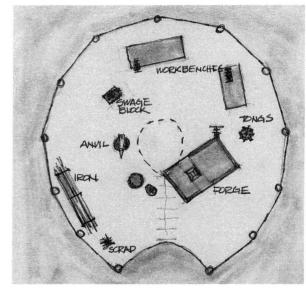

Layout of the equipment in the tipi.

8

at each location. The varying sizes of the circles and arrows indicate the relative values that I assigned to each piece of equipment. The general working relationships are illustrated here. This diagram can serve as a guideline for setting up your own equipment. (Since I am right-handed, the diagram is set up for those working right-handed as is the case throughout the book.) Most of your work will be done between the forge and the anvil. Each step that you save and each turn that you can shorten will be to your advantage. You may want to vary the distance from the forge to the anvil depending on the kind of work that you are doing. They can be close together when you are doing small pieces. but you will need more space when you are doing large pieces. Set up your forge and anvil first. Layout table, tool rack and other items can easily be moved.

When I worked in my tipi, I raked the earthen floor everyday before I started work. At the end of the day, I could see my footprints and my work patterns. The diagram of the work relationship was developed from this pattern. After working in the tipi for a while, I found that some of my right-angled arrangements were not very good, so I made some changes.

If you are visiting another smith and watching him or her work, try to see how the space is used and try to imagine how this would work for you. Watching the forming of hot metal is fun, but don't ignore the steps that the smith takes or their stance and posture. The way in which the tools are used by the smith is sometimes not apparent and often he or she will not be able to explain some subtle action. Observe, sketch and take notes.

I assume throughout this book that you will be working by yourself while you are learning forging. This means that you will be a single handed smith. The descriptions and exercises are selected with this in mind. Later, some of the exercises will call for a slightly different arrangement for your

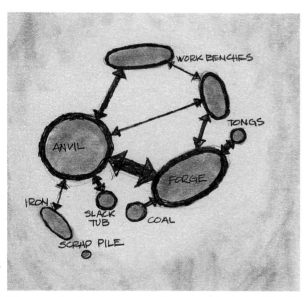

Diagram showing the amout of usage and relationship of tools and equipment.

equipment, because the striker, your helper, stands on the side of the anvil opposite the smith.

The other important features of a good smithy are: proper light, good ventilation and adequate storage.

Light

It should be fairly obvious that you need enough light to see the work that you are doing, but many smiths ignore this important consideration. Working in direct sunlight can be a problem. It is difficult to see the color of the hot metal and to ascertain the temperature.

If smiths would go to work and wash their windows, clean out behind their bellows, pick up the scrap that lies promiscuously about the shop, gather up the bolts, etc., they would be surprised at the change that it would make, not only in the general appearance of their shop, but also in the ease and convenience of doing work. One great disadvantage under which most smiths labor is the lack of light. Frequently blacksmith shops are stuck down in a basement or in some remote corner of a building. It is a fact, whether it be disregarded or not, that it is easier to do good work in a clean, well-lighted shop than in one which is dirty and dark.   [M. T. Richardson, *Practical Blacksmithing*, vol. I, p. 75]

Ventilation

Good ventilation is vital for your health. You must have a chimney and hood that draws properly. It will draw out the smoke and will help keep the ash from flying around. In addition, a good draft will help to keep the fire burning when you are doing other tasks.

There are two basic types of chimneys: one made of brick and the other of sheet metal and smoke pipe. Unless you are an experienced mason or smith, it is best to plan something simple. The hood may either be attached to or hung over the forge, depending on your preference, although the bell hood will not draw as well. Think about the ways in which the chimney will be affected by things outside it, such as the shape of the roof,

The Diamond Forge Tipi with prevaliling wind side rolled up providing ventilation and light.

adjacent buildings, trees and prevailing winds.

When you are setting up your forge, think about the flow of fresh air through the smithy. It is important that windows and doors be positioned to allow an even flow of cool air into the smithy.

Another important feature of the smithy is the floor. I have worked on concrete floors, but they are hard on the feet and legs. In addition, it is difficult to "set" your anvil and other equipment on a concrete floor. The dirt floor in my tipi was better on my legs and feet. The concrete floor is better for moving heavy equipment and working large pieces. It also needs little maintenance. About floors, Holmstrom says:

A plank floor is a great nuisance around the anvil. Every piece cut off hot is to be hunted up and picked up or it will set fire to it. I know there will be some objection to this kind of floor, but if you once learn how to keep it you will change your mind. To make this floor take sand and clay with fine gravel, mix with coal dust and place a layer where wanted about four inches thick. This floor, when a little old, will be as hard as iron, provided you sprinkle it every night with water. The dust and soot from the shop will, in time, settle in with it and it will be smooth and hard. It will not catch fire; no cracks for small tools or bolts to fall through; it will not crack like cement or brick floors. [J. G. Holmstrom, *Modern Blacksmithing*, p. 31]

Storage

Frequently you will wish you could remember where you placed a tool, test piece or a jig. Horizontal surfaces quickly become refuges for all kinds of implements. There are never enough flat surfaces, so provide as much storage as you can afford: tool and stock racks, sample and test piece shelving, cabinets and cases for flammable items along with the consideration for all of your other needs. As an example, considerable time can be saved in making a simple rack displaying your files—along with the fact that this saves the wear and dulling action of files banging around in a box.

To plan or design the ultimate workshop is difficult, if not impossible. Allow it to grow and develop over time. Set aside a time to think about the work and activity of the previous week and make changes that will make your work more pleasant and productive. Some smiths do this at the end of each project or job, others set aside some day of the week to get organized and do preventative maintenance. Find your own method, don't just go plunging ahead without taking time to reflect. To me, my shop is more than just a place to work—

It is something to be able to paint a picture, or carve a statue, and so to make a few objects beautiful. But is far more glorious to carve and paint the atmosphere in which we work, to effect the quality of the day. This is the highest of the arts.   [Henry David Thoreau]

Tools and Materials

The Anvil

The anvil is the king of tools for the blacksmith. Its design has been developed over centuries and there are thousands of different designs. Almost any type of anvil can be used to get started, but the preferred type of anvil is the "new style pattern." New anvils are expensive and generally the older anvils will be a good buy. Look around for a used one. (Unfortunately, collectors and antique dealers are also looking.)

There are several important things to look for when you are buying an anvil: the size, weight and general condition. Listen to the ring of the anvil when it is struck. Cran says:

The quality of an anvil can generally be judged by its "ring," a good anvil giving out a sharp, clear sound when struck with a hammer; if soft or not free from flaws, the sound will be dull. A good anvil mounted on a block in such a manner that it gives out its full volume of sound is easier to work upon than one where the ring is deadened. [James Cran, *Machine Blacksmithing*, p. 23]

Hit the anvil lightly and notice how the hammer responds. Does it jump back up or does it just lie there? The hammer is partially lifted by the life of the anvil. A lively anvil can make your work much easier. Forged anvils respond well; in contrast, cast-iron anvils have a tendency to be dead and full.

The main working parts of the anvil are the horn, the face and the edges; if these are not in good

New style anvil pattern.

shape, you will have problems. Examine the horn for excessive chisel marks or dents; if it is only lightly marred, the imperfections can be ground out. Check the face for sinks; if they are not too deep, you can work around them. If there are large, long chips on the outer edge, consider passing up the anvil.

Any used anvil is worn on the face. This is not always bad. My first anvil, 142 pounds, an "old style pattern," has a shallow but smoothly worn area on the face about one fourth of the way from the step. This slight depression is an advantage when I am straightening and bending, and most of the time, it is out of the way since I prefer to do most of my work about one-third to one-half the distance from the step.

Selecting an Anvil

To get started, buy an anvil that weighs between 100 and 170 pounds, depending on the type of work that you will be doing. When you are working single-handed and doing light work, a small anvil is sufficient, but when you are working with a striker, you need a heavier anvil. In general, it is better to have a heavier anvil than a lighter one. The weight of the old style anvil is described by the numbers on the side. It is an old system based on the hundredweight, one unit of which is equal to 112 pounds. The first number is in full hundredweight the second number is in quarters of hundredweight, and the third is in actual pounds. An anvil marked 116 is the sum of 112, 28 and 6, or 146 pounds.

The new-style anvils have their actual weight marked in pounds. The shape and proportions of the new style anvils are different than those of the old style, but the results are the same. Both anvils work equally well and the selection comes down to personal choice and availability.

The most important factor in purchasing a used anvil is the condition of the face and the edges.

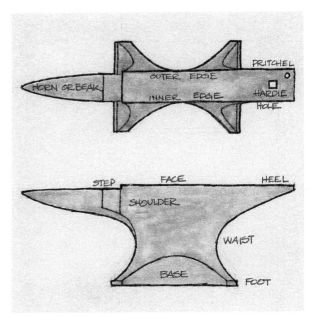

Plan and description of a new style anvil.

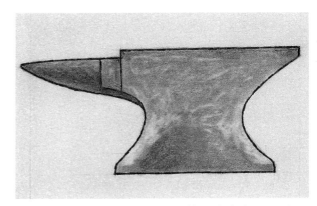

An old-style anvil pattern called a Mousehole because it was made in the Mousehole Forge in England.

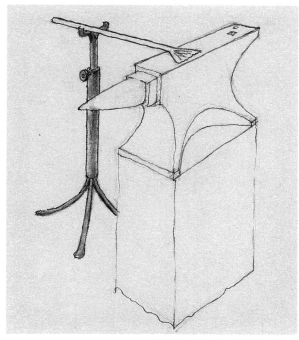

A stand used to hold work, called the blacksmith's helper.

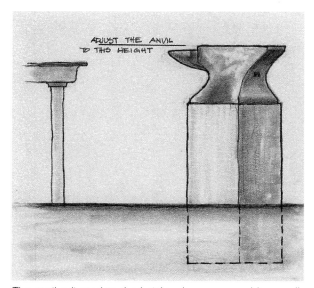

The anvil adjusted to the height where one would normally hold material to work on the face of the anvil.

Excessive pitting, chips on the edges and cracks in the face of the anvil are major problems. In some cases the chips or pits can be welded with the appropriate materials and redressed. If the face of the anvil, a piece of tool steel welded to the body, is badly cracked, it might be beyond repair.

The edges of a new anvil are usually sharp and should be dressed, which is grinding the edge to the proper radius. From the shoulder to the mid point develop the edge to 3/8-inch radius. Blend this radius into a 1/4-inch radius from the mid point to the heel. The edge of the heel can be either sharp or rounded. Some anvils have never had their edges dressed in this manner; as a result, they are easily chipped. Usually, new anvils have to be dressed out.

Sometimes a smith leaves a sharp edge on the heel of the anvil to bend a tight inside angle or to cut stock, instead of using the hardie. Be careful when you do this; it is potentially dangerous, because pieces of metal can easily be chipped from the edge of the anvil.

Setting the Anvil

"Setting the anvil" is mounting it in position. It is absolutely vital to have the anvil on a stand at the right height and distance from the forge. You will probably go through a bit of jockeying around to find the proper position and height, but once this has been established, it is best to anchor the stand to the floor or sink it into the floor. In general, you should be able to hold a piece of iron comfortably on the face of the anvil without bending over.

The simplest stand that you can make for the anvil is a heavy log of elm or other non-splitting wood. Sink the log into the ground a foot or more. This anchors it securely. Make sure that the anvil is held firmly to the stand. You can secure it with heavy staples. Other anvil stands can be fabricated from heavy lumber or angle iron and bolted to the floor.

The Forge

If the anvil is king, then the forge is the alchemist, for the forge contains the transforming fire. The fire transforms the metal into a plastic medium, making it easy to work and form. The fire also changes the crystalline structure of the metal, causing changes in its physical properties (later discussed in the section on "Metallurgy for the Blacksmith").

The forge is an open hearth where the smith makes his fire. It is made up of the tuyere and firebox, a hood and chimney, the hearth and the blower or bellows. Forges are made in a variety of configurations, some with side blast tuyeres as opposed to the bottom blast, some with hoods over the top of the hearth and others with the hood on the side next to the chimney. Small portable forges are usually found on farms, bottom blast with no hood. The Champion 400 is larger and good for general smithing, bottom blast with hood on the side and chimney above. The forge that I made to use in the tipi is built of 4 x 4 oak lumber with a new Buffalo firebox and tuyere, an old blower and a steel plate holding the hearth (which was firebrick and fireclay). The tipi acted as the hood and chimney and worked well. I bolted a post vise to the left-hand corner of the forge. This is an extremely handy arrangement, because it provides space for a large working area around the vise. There is also a small surface plate at this corner which doubled as a small anvil. It is convenient to have racks on the sides of the forge to hold tongs and other tools. Sometimes a coal bin and a water trough are built into the forge. A slack tub is needed, which is a large container of water placed close to the forge and anvil. A coal bucket and shovel are also handy.

Tuyere and Firebox

"Tuyere" is a French word derived from tuyau, meaning blowpipe. Through it, the blast of air enters the fire box, and creates the intense heat needed for forging. It controls the size and char-

The tipi forge.

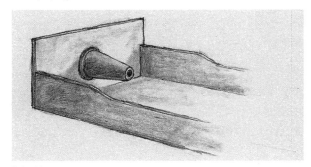

Side blast tuyere.

A small portable forge sometimes used for heating rivets on construction sites.

16

Tuyere opening	3/4"	1"	1-1/8"
Depth of firebox	4"	5"	6"
Supply pipe	1 3/4"	2"	2"
Size of work	1/4"	2"	2-4"

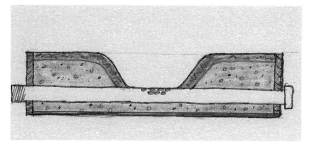

Sizes of parts for designing and constructing a primitive pipe forge fire box assembly.

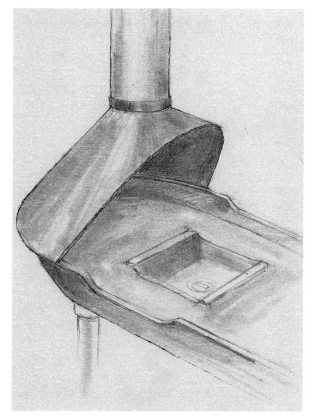

Section through a pipe forge.

Champion 400 hood and forge.

acter of the fire by its shape and the amount of air directed into the fire. The type of tuyere that is commonly used today was preceded by the side-blast tuyere, which was developed in Europe. The side-blast tuyere, which is separate from the firebox and ash dump, should be water-cooled to keep it from burning and clogging with clinkers.

The simplest of all tuyeres is a pipe with a series of holes in the middle. One end is plugged, the other is attached to the blower. It is installed so the fire is built over the hole.

The firebox is made of fireclay and firebrick. This is serviceable and gets you started, although there is no grate or ash dump. Use the following chart to act as a guideline in determining sizes for the forge and tuyere: the air pressure should be at least 6 to 10 ounces per square inch.

Cast iron assemblies of a tuyere, firebox and ash dump are readily available and easy to set up in a hearth. (See the "Resources" section.)

The hood is critical in directing the smoke into the chimney. Place the hood close to the hearth to catch the smoke and to help create a draft. Don't place it too high since it loses drawing power; if it is too large, it can get in the way of your work so a happy balance has to worked out. The chimney for the hood should be straight with as few bends in it as possible.

The blast (the air for the fire) is blown by a bellows or a mechanical blower and provides the oxygen needed to bring the fire to a high temperature. Today most smiths use an electric blower. It is important to be able to control the amount of air to the fire since this controls the rate of burn and temperature. The amount of air can be controlled with a suitable rheostat on the motor and/or a butterfly valve in the blast tube. An on/off switch for the air blast should be within easy reach, since you should cut the blast each time iron is taken from the fire to prevent burning up the fuel quickly. Usually, the blower is mounted on a shelf underneath the forge. It is then out of the way, but close to the tuyere. (A number of different types of blowers can be used.)

Slack Tub

Also associated with the anvil and forge is the slack tub, which is a water container. Water is used for coking the coal, cooling the iron and sometimes heat treating. It is important to have the slack tub close at hand and it is better to have a large slack tub for cooling large pieces of hot iron. Use a metal or wooden container since a plastic container can easily be burnt or punctured with the hot iron.

Workbench

You will be doing many different things at the workbench. It is important to have several things at hand: a bench grinder for dressing tools, wire brushes for cleaning and finishing, and a vise with related hand tools for finishing operations. Be sure that you have enough space to lay out drawings and complex parts for assembly.

There are many other tools that you will find handy: an assortment of files, a hacksaw, drills, a drill press, a band saw and other hand tools. The main thing to consider is the organization of these tools and the way in which they are used and stored, in much the same way that you consider the arrangement of the forge and anvil. Don Streeter summarized this problem of organization quite well in his book, *Professional Smithing:*

The need for speedy decisions leaves little room for disorganization. Tools required should be within reach, and those not needed should be out of the way. Enough clutter will develop with the best of intentions; tools that are used only occasionally are stored elsewhere. Because most of the work done here is small in size, no great space is required, so it is possible to move from forge to anvil or vise in a couple of steps. The anvil is so placed that when working the fire, one makes only a quarter turn to face the

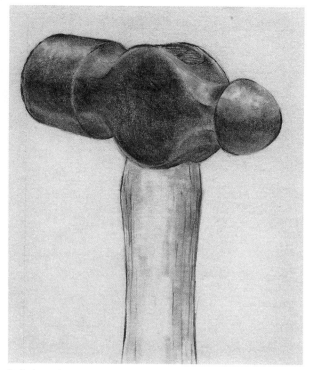

Ball peen hammer.

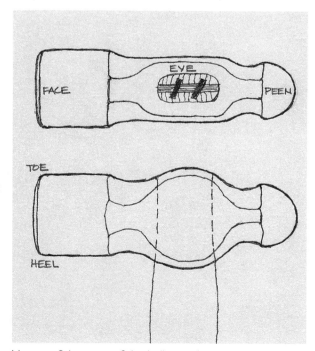

Names of the parts of the ball peen hammer.

anvil. This seems to be a more practical arrangement than having to make a complete about-face from one to the other, when more time is lost in making the move. This way, a turn of the head shows whether the anvil is clear and ready for work.

The Hammer

The hammer is the prince of the blacksmith's tools. In the pursuit of any other craft using materials that can be handled, such as clay, wood, leather or fiber, the craftsman feels the material. The hammer is of vital importance to the smith, because in blacksmithing, the smith feels the iron through the hammer.

The distinguishing characteristics of a hammer are the peen, which is the end of the head opposite the face, and the weight of the hammer. It is the shape of the peen which enables us to differentiate between different types of hammers. In general, a hammer that weighs between one and three pounds is adequate. You may occasionally need something lighter or heavier.

It would be difficult to describe all of the different types of hammers, since there are an incredible number of hammers that have been made for all of the varied arts, crafts and trades. Find them and use them; for "By the hammer and the hand all the arts do stand."

The head of the hammer is made of tool steel which has been heat-treated. The face and peen are hard and durable; in contrast, the body is tough, strong and resilient. When you are buying a new hammer, redress the face by grinding out the sharp edges. This prevents the hammer from marking the iron. The eye of the hammer holds the handle. Note the difference between the top of the eye and the bottom of the eye. The large wooden wedge expands the top of the handle to the sides and the small steel wedges tighten it securely.

Hammer handles are usually made of hickory because of its strength, long clean grain and resiliency. Sometimes ash or other woods are substituted. The handle must be securely attached and aligned at a right angle to the head. A faulty alignment can result in misdirected blows. The handle is fullest about two-thirds of the way down making this the most comfortable place to grip the handle. It is best to treat the handle with linseed oil which seals the wood. The wood has an open grain, allowing the oil to penetrate and ensuring a firm grip. Never varnish or lacquer the handle; it is much too slippery with a sweaty hand.

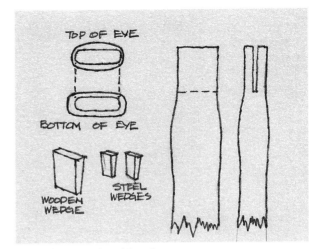

Parts of the head and handle.

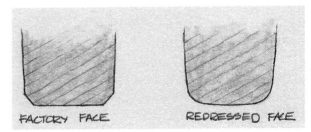

Cross sections of hammer heads.

Sledges

Sledges are heavier than hammers, and are used by the striker. The hand sledges (sometimes called the uphand sledge) weigh between 5 and 10 pounds. The swing sledges are heavier, up to 20 pounds, with longer handles. The striker does not raise the hand sledge over his head, as with the swing sledge which he swings like an ax in a full arc. The striker must be skillful to use the swing sledge effectively and safely. (See more on the striker in the section on "Heat Treating Tools.")

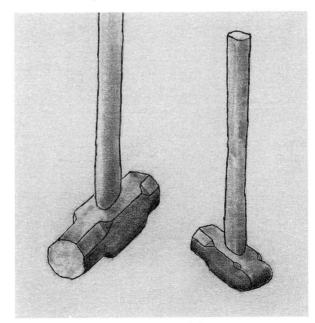

A double faced and a cross peen sledge.

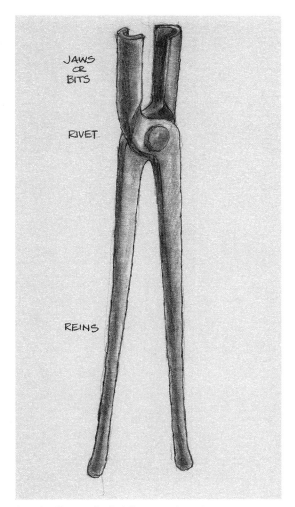

A pair of tongs for holding round stock.

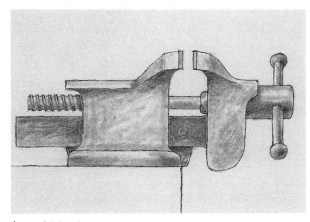

A machinist vise.

Tongs

Tongs are an extension of your hand. Plan your work so that the iron can be held in your hand. However, as the work progresses you must eventually cut off the piece and hold it with tongs. You probably will need more tongs than any other tool. Make an open tong rack within easy reach of the forge where you will be able to see all of your tongs with the "bits" up.

Tongs are referred to by the task that they perform or by the shape of the "jaws" or bits. For example, pickup tongs are used at the forge for picking up pieces in the fire, and are not generally used for holding iron while forging.

The handles are called "reins." If you slide a ring, or coupler, on the end of the reins and force it on tightly, you can grip the iron securely with the jaws of the tongs. This allows you to manipulate the tongs easily while maintaining a secure grip on the iron. You will need rings in several sizes.

Vise Grips and a variety of pliers always find uses. Vise Grips do a great job of holding punches and chisels. Round nose pliers are useful for holding and forming small pieces.

Vises

The vise is the third hand of the smith. There are two types of vises: the machinist vise or bench vise and the post vise, which is sometimes called a box vise or stake vise. The machinist vise is the most familiar as it is used to hold or clamp the metal when you are finishing a project or doing light work. Its jaws remain parallel during opening and closing. The post vise jaws hinge and so do not remain parallel. Both of the jaws are joined to the post; when a blow is struck, the force is transferred down the post to its foundation. The screw-thread assembly does not receive any of the hammering force and will not break as it might on a machinist vise. Mount the post vise securely on a heavy bench with a solid base, which absorbs the force of the blow.

At times, the jaws of a vise will be too sharp and mar the piece being held. To prevent this make two pads for the jaws from 1/4-inch mild steel plates. Heat up one plate at a time and clamp in the vise and bend over with a sledge; then bend the second pad. Aluminum angles may also be used as pads to hold pieces and keep delicate pieces from being damaged. Cut off the angles to the width of the vise jaws and hammer form to fit.

When you are looking at old post vises, look at the screw assembly. Examine the screw and hemispherical washer for excessive wear. These are difficult to repair. If the spring that holds the jaws open is missing, a new one can be made. A new holding or mounting plate can also be made, if necessary.

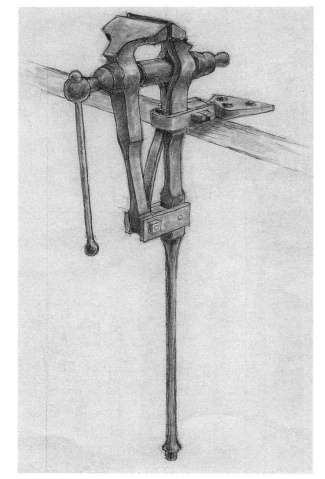

The blacksmith's post vise.

Anvil Tools

The anvil tools, that is, tools which are used in the anvil, make up the court of the king. These tools have square shanks which fit into the square hole, the hardie hole, near the tail of the anvil. A good fit of the tool in the hardie hole is imperative because this keeps the tool from jumping around when struck.

Hardies and Sets

The hardie is the anvil tool that is used most often. In use, they are placed in the hardie hole or in a vise. Hardies are used to cut hot or cold metal and they can have either a curved or straight edge. Iron can be cut off flush or beveled with the hardies.

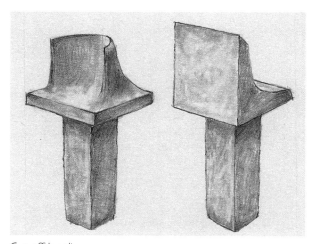

Cut off hardies.

22

The hardie is a bottom tool. It has a mate which does the same job, but which is held on the top of the piece. The hardie's mate is a chisel and is called the top tool. The top tool may or may not have a handle. The ones with handles are called either hot or cold sets (or sate). They are always struck with a sledge, and are never swung like a hammer. The purpose of this handle is to prevent burning yourself and to keep your hand from being hit with a hammer or sledge. The handles are straight pieces of wood and are set without wedges, since they are frequently broken with a missed sledge blow. The old handles can then just be hammered back into place.

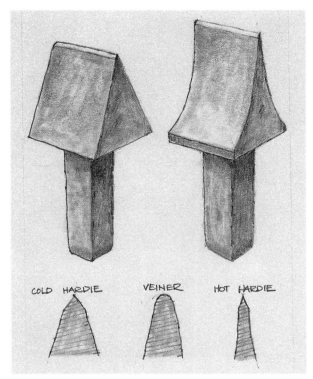

COLD HARDIE VEINER HOT HARDIE

Cold and hot hardies with profiles of their cutting edges.

Top and bottom tools can be used singly or as matched pairs. When top and bottom tools are used together, that is opposing one another, they form or cut iron easily and quickly.

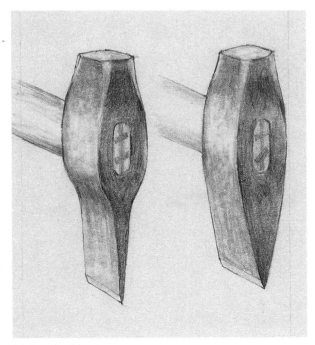

Hot and cold sets.

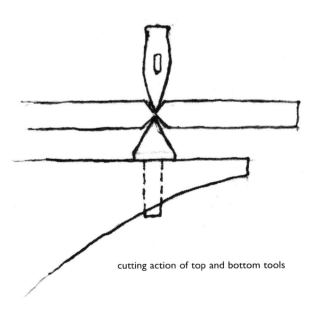

cutting action of top and bottom tools

Fullers

The top and bottom fullers are used to spread metal in a horizontal direction, in other words, to reduce the cross section. They are basic forming tools that act just like your fingers when you are squeezing clay. Used together or singly they start many initial forming operations in forging. The cheese fuller is used to spread, as well as to make bends.

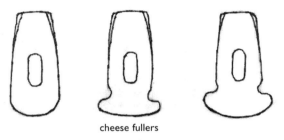

cheese fullers

Swages

Swages are forming tools used to shape and finish the iron. You can make swages to create any desired cross section of metal. The spring swage is a good example. The spring swage is useful to the single-handed smith, the iron can be held in one hand while the hammer can be used to strike the swage. This type of swage can be made to fit in the hardie hole or the jaws bent at a 90° angle which facilitates holding both the piece of iron and the swage at the same time.

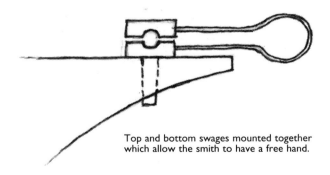

Top and bottom swages mounted together which allow the smith to have a free hand.

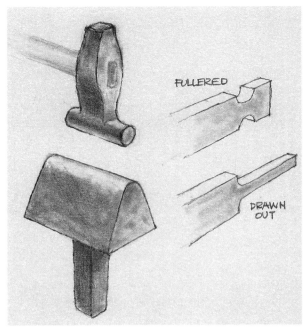

FULLERED

DRAWN OUT

A top and bottom fuller with a fullered and drawn out section of iron

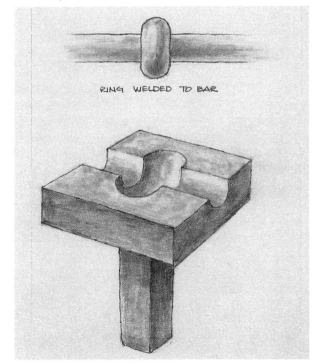

RING WELDED TO BAR

A bottom swage used with a matching top swage used to forge weld a ring on a bar.

Swage Block

The swage block is a versatile bottom tool that is sometimes called a swage anvil. It can be used in two positions: lying down or standing on one of its sides. Use the holes for heading, bending, shaping and forming.

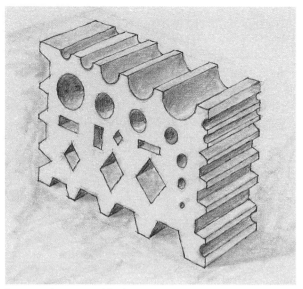

Rectangular swage block.

Flatter

The flatter or flattie, is the tool which is struck to flatten or to smooth out the surface of the metal when there are dents and other imperfections.

Flatter.

Set Hammer

The set hammer is to used form metal in tight areas where a direct hammer blow is difficult to make. It has a sharp or a shaped edge to form corners, shoulders and other forms. For more accurate control the set hammer is "set" into position and then struck with a sledge or hammer.

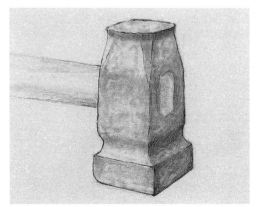

Set hammer.

Punches and Bolsters

Punches are used to punch round, square, oval or just about any shaped hole. You can make the punch shape and sizes as needed. The final blow of punching a hole is usually done over the hardie hole or the pritchel hole. A bolster is used if the punch is too large for the hardie hole; it is placed under the iron which allows the punch to penetrate the iron. Bolsters are of different diameters and shapes, about 1-inch thick.

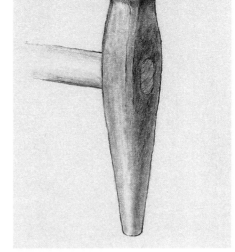
Round punch.

Repoussé and Chasing Tools

Repoussé and chasing tools are used in sheet metal work and are the basis for the forming process which can be called "repoussé." Repoussé shapes the piece, initially forming bulges from the back of the metal. Chasing is working on these bulges, from the front, to give definition to the design. The basic tools are:

1. Tracers are sharp-edged chisels, either thin or blunt, used to trace the design on the back of the metal. The profile of tracers have rounded corners to prevent breaking through the metal.
2. Modeling tools are tools used to work down the metal from the front. The edges of these tools are rounded to various radii.
3. Punches are used to indent their shape into the metal and are curved, flat, angled, circular and pointed.
4. Matting and graining tools are used to texture a surface and can be made in a wide variety of textures.

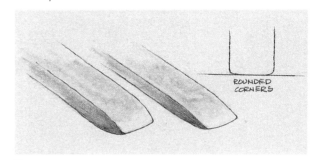
Tracers.

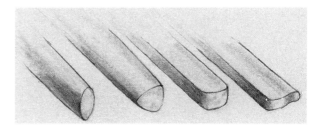
Modeling tools for chasing.

Matting tools for texturing.

26

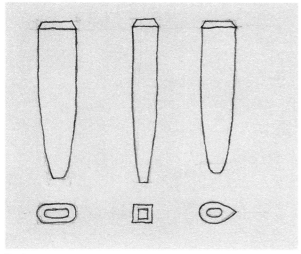

Drifts.

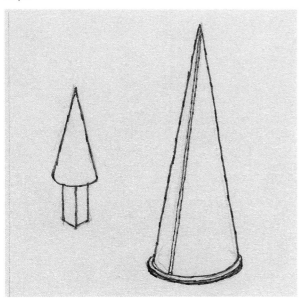

Anvil and floor mandrel.

Rivet set and cupping tool.

Drifts

A drift is used in a hole to open and form it to particular shape. A common drift is an oval-shaped drift which is used to shape the eye for a hammer. Drifts can be left in place while the hammer head is being forged. Since they will get hot when used this way, they are best made of a heat resisting steel.

Mandrel

Mandrels are used to form circular shapes and rings. The small mandrel fits into the hardie hole. When this small mandrel is bent over at an angle, it is called an anvil beak, because it is a smaller version of the beak on the anvil. It is frequently shaped like a small anvil. The larger cone mandrel weighs 100 pounds or more and stands on the floor.

Rivet Tools

The cupping tool is a finishing tool used to clean up the head of a rivet. The companion to the cupping tool is the rivet set, which is placed on the bottom side of the rivet being formed so that it will not be flattened.

Header

A heading tool is used to make heads on nails and bolts. It is a bar of tool steel with one or more tapered holes of different sizes. A bolt header has a flat face whereas the hole on the nail header has a raised face. This makes it easy to finish the head of the nail with angled blows.

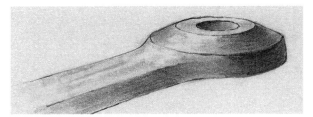

Bolt header which could also be used to make large nails as below.

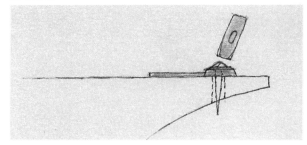

Nail header in use.

Twisting Wrenches

Twisting wrenches provide the balance and leverage for twisting heavy sections of iron. You can use small adjustable pliers, pipe wrenches or Vise Grips to twist small pieces of metal, but since they have only one handle, the twisting action is not balanced. To prevent this wobble in the twist, use two pair of these smaller wrenches.

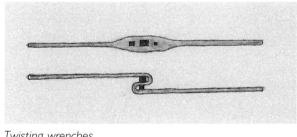

Twisting wrenches.

Saddles

A saddle, or a bridge, is used to form the jaws of open-ended wrenches, the tines on forks, and other forms when the horn of the anvil is unsuitable or too thick.

The cutting saddle, or cutting plate, is used to split or cut iron when the piece is too large for the step of the anvil. The first cuts are made on the face of the anvil or step of the anvil as it is a more solid base. When the chisel has almost penetrated the metal, the piece is moved to the saddle to finish the cut. This saves the chisel and the face of the anvil. Aluminum and copper are used for cutting saddles since the softer metals absorb the blows and does not bounce as much as a steel saddle.

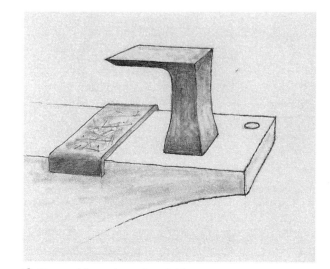

Cutting saddle and an open bridge.

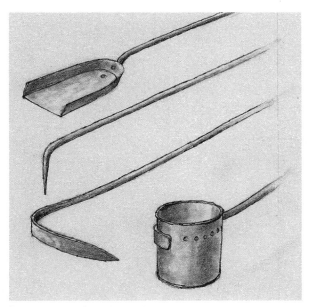

Shovel, poker, fire rake and watering can.

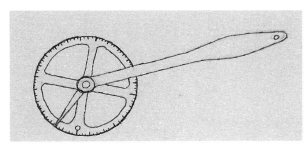

Traveler.

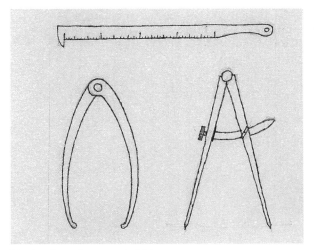

Hook rule, calipers and dividers.

Fire Tools

Tools used at the forge are called either fire or forge tools. The most common are the poker, rake, shovel and watering can. Stands and supports are used at the anvil and the forge to hold the work, leaving the tong hand free. They are sometimes called the "second man" or the "blacksmith's helper." (See page 15.)

Measuring Tools

Measuring tools at the forge should be made of metal so they do not burn. The hook rule is handy. You can measure hot iron easily by hooking the tip over the end of the iron. Use chalk or a soapstone pencil for general marking, but when you want to mark a piece that will be placed in the fire, use a center punch or a chisel to incise a fine line. Calipers are used to check the thickness of iron as it is being forged. Travelers are used to measure larger pieces; they have a circumference of one to two feet. To measure a piece, roll the traveler along the piece and count the revolutions.

Coal

The formation of coal takes eons of time. The process begins with the growth of plants, dying and accumulating which become peat, which in turn is gradually compressed into coal. It is estimated that it takes three feet of peat to make a seam of bituminous coal one foot thick. Under the proper conditions, the peat goes through the following stages as it is transformed into coal: peat, brown coal, lignite, sub-bituminous, bituminous, semi-anthracite and anthracite. We are concerned only with bituminous coal which weighs around 45 pounds per cubic foot. A dry analysis of bituminous coal ranges as follows:

Ash	7-11 percent
Fixed carbon	60-78 percent
Volatile matter	11-33 percent

By looking at this analysis, you can see that only 7 to 11 percent of the material does not burn; this forms the ash and clinker. Coke is the desired fuel for the smith. To make coke, you drive off the volatile matter in the form of smoke. It is burnt as it comes from the fire. This process is called coking, and it is done at every work session at the forge. The coke made at the forge is called "breeze," since it is light and easily broken apart. In contrast, metallurgical coke is heavier and difficult to break apart. It is made basically for the steel industry. It is a excellent fuel, particularly when welding. However, it is more difficult to start and maintain a fire with this type of coke.

You can easily break blacksmithing coal apart in your hands. Examine it for white flakes or brown and yellow spots; these are impurities and sulfur, respectively. The pieces of coal should be no larger than a dime and contain about 20% to 30%of "fines." Fines is the coal dust and is important in cementing the mass of coal together as coke. (You may have noticed by now the linguistic shorthand that the blacksmith uses: "flattie," "heading tool," "breeze" and "fines." These terms are direct and delightfully simple.) To summarize, your coal should have little ash, be high-bituminous, be the correct size, be free from sulfur and have the right amount of fines mixed with it.

You can check the coal when it is burning by examining the color of the flame; it should be a bright, clean, light orange glow. The bed of the fire should be a uniform color without hot spots. If the fire has hot spots and "drops out," that is, burns out rapidly, then the coal is questionable for forging purposes. Examine the coke around the edges of the fire; it should be solid and be a clean, dark gray color. If it is not, it is dirty.

Metallurgical coke is made from the best grades of bituminous coal for the iron and steel industry. It is different from the breeze that you make in your forge; it is hard and difficult to break up for the fire. It is a great fuel that burns clean and hot and should be considered for use.

Charcoal was the first fuel used by smiths. It is sometimes used today when a lower temperature and a clean fire are desired. It is lighter than coal and can easily be blown out of the firebox by the blast. Charcoal can be used when working with high carbon steels to prevent them from being decarburized.

Gas

Natural gas and LP or propane gas are being used by an increasing number of smiths today. They are excellent alternative sources of heat for forging. Propane can be found in portable cylinders from 11 to 100 pounds. Natural gas is not as widely available in rural areas, but is readily available in urban areas. Gas is clean burning without smoke, dust or clinkers; it is reliable, easy to control and is readily obtainable. There are many sources of kits and ready made gas furnaces and gas forges. You must know the safety requirements and the technique for working with gas furnaces. Go to a workshop or work with someone who has the experience before striking out on your own.

Gas Fired Forge Furnace

The term forge furnace describes a forge in which the heating chamber is almost completely contained by a ceramic lining to control the atmosphere, to keep the heat in and to keep scaling to a minimum. Forge furnaces can be constructed for the size of work planned and can be fairly light weight and compact. They offer the possibilities of controlled temperatures, few environmental problems, versatility and portability.

The ability to easily see the work in the heat chamber and have multiple pieces ready to forge makes the gas fired furnaces efficient and productive. The negative aspects of these furnaces is that they are difficult to operate at less than 1800°F. which makes them somewhat unsuitable for heat treating. Also, the scale formed on iron in a gas fire is harder and more difficult to remove.

The cost of operating a gas fired forge furnace will vary with the size and capacity of the heat chamber, the materials with which it is constructed and the number of burners used. An average sized two burner furnace with ceramic board lining can be operated for around $1.00 per hour with the LP cost of $1.00 per gallon.

The interior of the heat chamber can be made from commercially available materials. Fire brick is made in temperature ranges from 1800°F. to 3700°F. and is often used in the floor of the chamber because of it's abrasion resistance and endurance when exposed to welding fluxes. Ceramic fiber board (available to 3600°F.) and castable refractory materials are used for the walls, roof and burner nozzles because they heat up quickly and are more reflective of the infrared radiation. The burning gas does not heat the work directly, but rather the reflected heat from the refractory lining does.

There are three major types of gas burners. The first is the "forced air burner" which uses a variable speed fan to force the air into a nozzle where it is mixed with gas and is blown into the burn chamber. Sometimes it is noisy and difficult to adjust to provide a reducing atmosphere in the forging furnace. The second is the "atmospheric burner" which uses combustion air sucked in through a bell shaped housing by the stream of gas flowing out of a small orifice. This type of burner makes less noise than the forced air model but requires higher minimum gas pressure to operate. The third is the "recuperative burner" which utilizes the exhaust forge heat to preheat the combustion air as it is blown through a heat exchanger before it mixes with the gas. The result is a hotter less oxidizing fire with reduced fuel consumption. Open hearth gas forges may be easier to use but scale the work heavily, have tremendous heat loss and are noisy.

Safety in gas fired forge furnace design, construction and operation is of primary consideration. A variable gas pressure regulator and a positive shut-off valve are required equipment. Adequate ventilation to remove carbon monoxide and to prevent oxygen depletion in the closed shop must be carefully considered. Other safety details to consider are safe ignition procedures, handling of LP gas and your local gas codes.

Ferrous Metals

Iron in its natural state is in the form of iron oxides. Pig iron is the iron that is extracted by means of a pyrochemical process in the blast furnace. Other iron products such as wrought iron, cast iron and steel, are made from pig iron. For a good understanding of these processes read *The Making, Shaping and Treating of Steel,* by U. S. Steel.

Iron alloys, basically steel, are the metals that the blacksmith forges. When placed in the fire, these oxidize rapidly, forming a layer of black scale. The blacksmith is so named because of this black oxide and is one of the positive attributes of the iron. It gives ferrous metals a dark rich patina when polished, which offers a contrast between the bright polished metal. At an orange heat (1740°F.) the scale can be readily brushed off with a wire brush.

At light cherry (1550°F.) and below, the scale adheres and the iron remains black; "hammer finishing" to develop smooth surfaces is best done at this temperature range. A "heat" refers to each time that a piece of iron is heated in the forge. The scale formed during each heat amounts to about 1 percent of the total weight of the iron. It is easy to see that you can lose much of your iron if you use an excessive number of heats. A good smith does the work required in as few heats as possible.

Wrought iron is 99% pure iron and is best described as a two-component metal consisting of high-purity iron and iron silicate, a particular type of glass-like slag. This slag is used to oxidize out the impurities in the pig iron from which it is made. The iron and the slag are in physical association, as contrasted to the chemical or alloy relationship that generally exists between the other metals. Wrought iron is the only ferrous metal that contains siliceous slag.

Wrought iron, also called "puddled iron," is so called because during the process of its manufacture, it is forged, or wrought, with large hammers to combine the slag with the iron. The amount of siliceous slag in wrought iron varies from 1 to 3 percent by weight. This slag gives wrought iron its fibrous character. You can determine whether a piece is wrought iron by nicking it with a cold chisel and bending it. There are fibers (like the fibers in wood) in the wrought iron, rather than grains which you would find in steel. Wrought iron is resistant to corrosion because of the purity of the iron and because of the protective properties of the slag. It is easier to forge and weld wrought iron than any of the other iron alloys, because it can be worked at higher heat. It is worked at a yellow heat (2100-2200°F.) and welded at a white heat (2500°F.). While wrought iron is still made in Europe, unfortunately it is no longer made in the United States. There are no commercial supplies of it available today. Scout around for it at a scrap yard, or when old buildings are demolished. However, it is best to plan on working with mild steel.

Steel is an alloy of iron and carbon; it usually contains varying degrees of manganese, phosphorus, sulfur and silicon. There is a long list of other alloys that can greatly vary the properties of the steel, called "alloy steels." (See "Metallurgy for the Blacksmith" for more information.) Carbon, however, is the major alloy of iron. The amount of carbon in the steel will range from a trace to about 1.70%. In the language of the blacksmith, this would be 170 points of carbon. Thus a point is 0.01%. A 1% carbon steel would have 100 points of carbon, and a 0.45% steel would have 45 points.

Steels are graded by the amount of carbon they contain. A simplified classification is:

Mild or low carbon steel	1-40 points
High carbon steel	40-60 points
Spring steel	70-80 points
Tool steel	80-170 points

Alloy steels are steels that contain elements other than carbon as their major alloying elements. They have enhanced physical properties as the result of these alloys. There is a more complete discussion of iron and steel in the section "Metallurgy for the Blacksmith."

Hereafter, in order to make things simple, the generic name of iron is used when the various techniques and processes are described. When a specific alloy is required for a task or tool, that name is used.

Safety

Before starting to work, one should be aware of a vital aspect—safety. There are many potential dangers associated with blacksmithing. Safety is a factor that should constantly be a part of your working habits.

Your eyes must be protected. I highly recommend that you wear safety glasses with side shields. Hot scale and chips of steel can severely burn and damage your eyes. The light radiation from a welding fire has large amounts of ultraviolet and infrared rays which are serious hazards. Use good safety glasses that will filter out the UV infrared rays.

The ring of the anvil and other loud noises in the smithy can cause hearing loss. I also strongly recommend the use of ear plugs or some form of ear protection. A single ring of the anvil does no damage, but repeated rings and noise will cause damage over time. Repetition of a sound, or breathing noxious fumes, or looking into welding fires or a continuous hammer motion can all cause damage. It is the constant repetition on a long term basis that causes damage.

Do not wear synthetic clothing while you are working, since it catches fire or melts quickly. Loose cotton clothing is better. A hat may be needed, a selection of leather gloves, a cotton or leather apron to protect yourself against some of the heat and dirt. Some smiths wear only a half apron.

A loose fitting leather glove can be worn on your tong hand when you are holding tongs, hot metal or tools. But find a good fitting glove if using a glove on your hammer hand, since you require good control and should not lose the feel of the hammer. Harden your hand with work. The only synthetic material that will withstand the high heat of the forge fire is

Kevlar; use gloves made of this material for picking up or holding hot items. A word of caution: if you are used to wearing gloves, you may forget one time and pick up hot iron. Think always of where that hot iron is!

Heavy duty, high-topped shoes with leather soles are important. The last time I wore low-cut shoes in the forge, a hot slug from a punched hole dropped into my shoe. I thought it was a bee at first and slapped it. I recommend that your shoes come up under your pants to protect you and provide good support.

Getting Started

By the time you have all of the tools just surveyed, your forge will be well equipped, but you can get started with just a few tools. This is a beginning shop, so collect your tools as you start to do some projects. Then you will have a much better idea of what you need. Though not necessary to begin, two power tools will come in handy: a drill press and a bench grinder.

First of all, establish where you are working and begin to plan the space. As you gather tools and the equipment, place them and check out the working relationships. Plan for the forge, since it is the largest piece of equipment and most difficult to set. Work out the ventilation and light. When you place the anvil and set it on its stand, do it properly, to avoid the frustration of having it slide around. Now plan for other large pieces of equipment.

You will need several hammers to begin with: a ball peen weighing around 1 1/2 pounds and a cross peen that is slightly heavier, around 2 pounds. A couple of pairs of tongs (to grip 1/4- to 1/2-inch stock) are helpful in the beginning; you can add more later. Vise grips and pliers fill in the gaps initially. A hardie, a number of chisels and several punches are vital.

Good coal is absolutely necessary, as are a bucket and shovel for the coal. A slack tub (water bucket) should be close to the forge. Visit the steel scrap yards and scrounge the countryside for steel. To start, try to get 1/4-inch, 3/8-inch and 1/2-inch rounds and squares, and then stockpile other sizes. Axles, coil and leaf springs from old cars are very useful for making some of your first tools.

With this abbreviated list you can fire up and start. You will quickly learn how to use these tools and evaluate what other tools and equipment you will want or need later.

Forging Processes

Lighting a Fire

The next step is to light the forge fire and your inner fire. Light these fires with the feeling that each time you forge you will learn something new. Keep these fires burning, supply fuel for them and tend them well. There may be discouraging periods that seem to weaken these fires; they are nothing more than clinkers. Once they are removed and replaced with new fuel, the fire will burn brighter than before

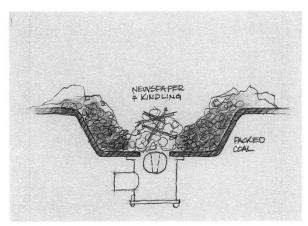

Sectional drawing of a fire box prepared to start a fire.

The first time you light a fire you have to make coke (breeze). Pack a layer of wet green coal around the sides of the firebox. (Green coal is new, unburnt coal.) Then place some wadded newspaper and small kindling in the center. Light the paper and use a slight blast of air to get the fire going. Add a few more pieces of wood as the fire catches. When the wood catches, place some more coal around the edges and a few pieces in the center of the fire. Do not smother the fire with green coal or you will be smothered with smoke. The coal will soon catch on fire and begin to burn off the volatile gases. Keep the air blast going. (Notice that the flame consumes the smoke; cut the blast and watch what happens.) Gradually build up the banks of green coal on the sides and back of the fire, wet down all of the coal with the watering can and pack down the banks with a shovel. This packing and watering with the fire forms coke. The fines in the coal acts like a cement to bind together the larger pieces. (This is the same process as making charcoal from wood.)

By now you should have a good fire and some coke. Cut the blast and check the fire with a poker. If the coal is sticking together on the sides it is coke. If not turn on the blast, pack the banks in closer to the center of the fire, and water it down again.

If you water down a new fire that has a lot of green coal in it, and do not have the blast on, it can cause a "blow back." This is a dull pop or explosion of the unburned gases that have been trapped in the firebox. This might not damage a blower, but could split an older bellows. It is not good practice, so always turn on the air blast before making coke.

Each time you shut down, make certain you have enough coke set aside to start another fire. In time you will need only a little paper or wood shavings with the saved coke to start a fire. Your first fire should be the last fire that has a lot of smoke. Good smiths are known by the way they start, maintain, bank and shut down a fire—something to work on.

Remove the ash and clinkers that form as the fire burns. A clean fire is essential. Cut the blast and gently dig around in the fire with the poker. Try to remove the entire clinker in one piece with the poker and pick-up tongs. Coke and coal will feel soft, but a clinker feels hard and clinks against the poker. Clinkers are the darker areas (holes) in the fire. Rotate the fire grate or tumbler several times and dump the ashes. It is important to turn off the blast from the blower when dumping ashes. Move the bank of coke and coal closer to the center of the fire with the shovel or fire rake and turn on the blast. Add more green coal to the outer edge of the bank and wet it down. You now have a good fire, which heats the iron more quickly. Build your fire to suit the size of the parts that you will be forging; keep the fire as small as possible.

There are three types of fires: reducing, neutral

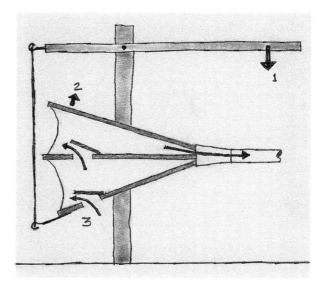

The double lung bellows operates by (1) pulling the lever down which closes the lower lung flap and forces air into the upper lung. (2) This raises the top board which then lowers forcing air through the pipe into the tuyere. (3) As the lever is lowered air flows into the lower lung starting the cycle over again.

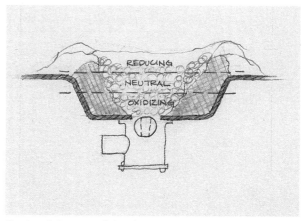

Sectional drawing of the three zones in a fire.

38

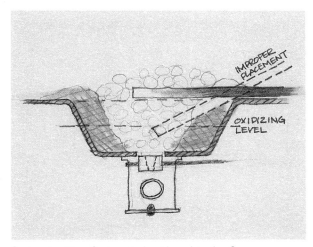

Proper position for iron to be placed in the fire.

and oxidizing. The reducing fire is one that consumes all of the oxygen from the blast. It is a compact bed of coals and coke. The sides and top are well banked and formed, so that the heat is reflected inward, making a hotter and more desirable fire. The oxidizing fire has excess oxygen. It is usually hollow, with burnt out spots and with bits of ash and clinker. It is impossible to weld in this type of fire and it is also more difficult to heat the metal, since it is not a hot fire. In a reducing or neutral fire, scale forms and about 1 percent of the metal's weight is lost in each heat. In an oxidizing fire, this loss is much greater. Proper fire maintenance is not difficult. Keeping the blast low and cutting it off just before removing the work from the fire is a big help. It takes time, but it saves time. Get in the habit of working with a good, clean fire.

Place the steel in the fire in a horizontal position with a good bed of coals under it. It will heat easily and have less tendency to scale (oxidize) because the oxygen is burnt off before it reaches the metal. In contrast, if you shove the steel down into the fire the metal will scale more, since it is placed in the oxidizing part of the fire. As a fire burns it can develop a hollow spot and this is also oxidizing. Check for a clinker and then push fuel down in the hollow to bring the fire back.

Cutting

The first piece that you work on is made from 1/4 or 3/8-inch round mild steel. Cut it off cold. Place the cold cut hardie in the anvil and place the piece across the edge of the hardie. Using a hammer strike the steel with direct, heavy blows. After several blows, rotate it and hit it on the other side. Notice the notches or nicks forming. When you are almost through the piece, slack off on your blows. The last blows seem mushy and you can feel the metal give. Stop. Do not try to cut all the way through, since you might hit the hardie's edge and damage it. Now bend and break it in your hands, or use the pritchel hole to snap it off.

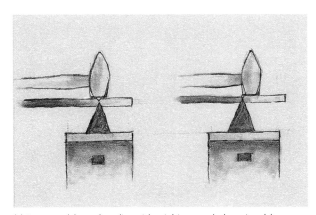

Using a cold cut hardie with nicking and shearing blows.

To cut a hot piece, place the bar in the fire and turn on the blast. Bring it to an orange heat. Always cut the blast when you remove a piece from the fire, this conserves fuel. Place the iron on the hot cut hardie and cut off an 18-inch piece. Use medium blows; notice how much easier it is to cut and how quickly the notches form. Slack off on your blows when you see a thin dark line appear on the bar where is thinnest. This is caused by the cooling action of the edge of the hardie. There are several ways to finish now: use shearing blows off the hardie or edge of the anvil; hold the piece on the face of the anvil and bend back and forth; or cool the piece in the slack tub and break it off. (The water hardens the metal, allowing it to snap off easily. Do not use this method for tool steels.) A shearing blow can also be used, but the piece can fly off—use care.

Heat the end of this piece of iron to heats ranging from yellow at the end to a dark red. Then strike the bar with the heel of the hammer with blows of equal force at intervals along the bar. Feel the difference in how the iron responds to the hits. Cool the bar and examine the difference in the hammer marks.

A quick method to find the center and cut a bar in half is to balance the bar on the edge of the hardie; cut at that point.

Drawing Out

The first forging process is to draw a taper in a bar. Place in the fire and bring to an orange heat the 18-inch piece that you have just cut off. While the iron is heating, think about what has to be done in preparation to forge the taper. Remove the hardie from the anvil and brush the scale from the anvil. Pick up your hammer. Cut the blast and remove the bar from the fire. Place it over the edge of the anvil. Check your stance and position at the anvil. Strike the piece with medium blows and gradually pull it back over the edge of the anvil. These blows

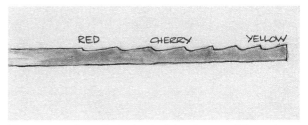

Hammer marks with the heel of the face at different heats.

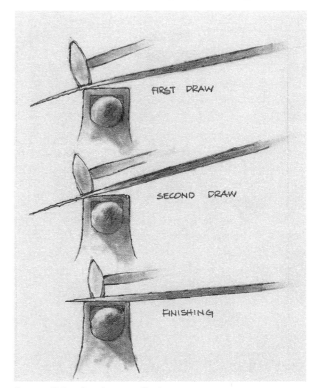

Steps of the drawing out forging process.

Drawing out over the beak of the anvil.

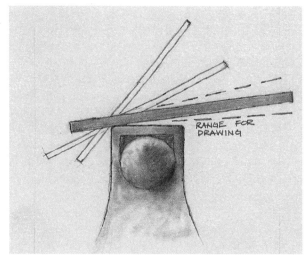

Range of the angle for drawing out over the edge or the anvil, as show between the dashed lines.

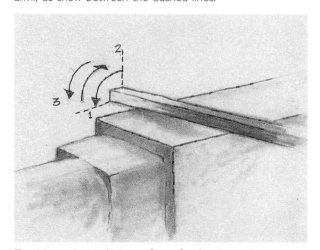

Tumbling a heated piece of iron for drawing out.

will cause the iron to bend and will create a dimpling effect on the bottom. Rotate the piece 180° and do the same thing to the other side. This straightens out the piece. Rotate it 90° and do the same thing to the other sides. The bar will be losing its heat by now, so place it flat on the face of the anvil, using light blows straighten it out and return it to the fire. Bring the piece to an orange heat and continue to draw out, concentrating on the end, which will come to a sharp point. Occasionally, lay it flat on the face of the anvil and hit flat blows to smooth out the dimples that have formed. Be careful not to let the dimples get too high or pointed.

Heat the taper again and prepare to finish it. Remember—Think in the fire and work when the iron is hot. Draw out the taper on the face of the anvil, continuing to work as the piece loses its heat until it is dark red. This is the finishing heat. Scale will not form now and some of the scale that has already adhered is removed by hammering the piece. Be careful to use light finishing blows. This is the heat at which a fine surface can be developed. You should not try to shape the metal at this heat since it is now losing its plastic quality. This is particularly true when working tool steels; working them at this heat might crack the steel.

Cool the taper and place the other end in the fire and prepare to taper it by "tumbling." Rotate the piece 90° on the edge of the anvil after the first blow. Then rotate it 90° back to the original position and strike it. This makes drawing out faster and easier. Develop a cadence or rhythm to your blows. (A good smith can be heard as well as seen.)

Bring the piece to the proper heat and place it over the edge of the anvil; hit and rotate, hit and rotate, hit and rotate. Do this until the end is reached. Then change the position of the bar in your hand, so that you strike the other two sides. Develop a square taper as before and finish off.

This is the basic operation of drawing out. You will use it many times. To ensure drawing out properly, dress the edge of the anvil as discussed in section on "Tools and Materials."

Pig Tail Hook

You can make hooks with the tapers that you have just finished. Heat a piece to light cherry; be careful, because the thin end heats more quickly and can easily burn. Start the bending blows as in (a) and continue as in (b) and (c). This forms a small pigtail or loop on the end. The heat will soon be lost on the thin section. Turn the piece over and proceed to step (d). Form a right angle as in (e), and take care to strike the hook at position (1) not at (2), as this thins the corner and weakens it. Now heat the piece to a light cherry, turn it over again and bend it over the beak of the anvil (f) with successive blows. (After you remove the piece from the fire, dip the pigtail in the slack tub. This cools the end, and you can hit it lightly with the hammer without deforming it.) You can make any size hook, depending on the radius of the anvil where the hook is placed and how your blows close the hook.

Heat the hook to cherry red and cut off the hook on the hardie about 1-inch from the right-angle bend. Holding the hook in a pair of suitable tongs, return it to the fire and draw a short taper for the nail end.

While the hook is still warm, rub it with an old candle or a piece of wax, then wire brush it. Place it over the fire to warm up again and rub it with wax again. The heat allows the wax to melt and to penetrate under the scale which acts as a moderate rust preventative. Rub the hook with a cloth after the hook cools. When you install the hook, drill a lead hole into the wall and then hammer the shank in. Notice that the pig tail cannot be higher that the shank; this would prevent the hook from being driven into the wall.

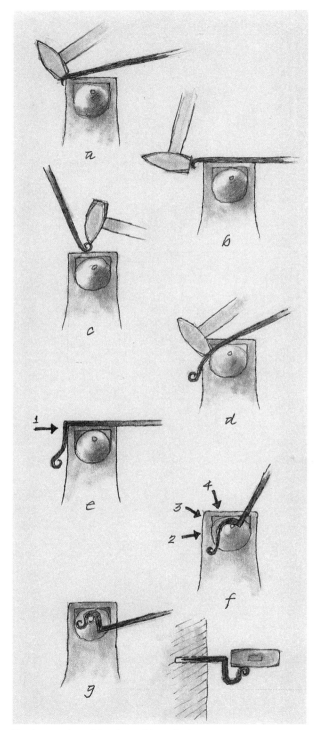

Forging a pig tail hook and installation.

42

It is important to follow this sequence of steps. There is usually an orderly procedure for each operation, although this is not immediately apparent. Always plan the sequence in advance, particularly for complex parts. Examine your hook. lt is your first piece. Note the qualities that you like and enhance those in your next hook.

The first steel that you worked with was light so get a heavier piece and try a hook that is heavier. Proceed through the same drawing-out steps to develop the square taper. Instead of using the edge of the anvil to draw out this time, use the beak of the anvil. Obviously it has a much larger radius and gives a different effect. It has a much different sound and response to the hammer, because it does not have the same mass as the body of the anvil.

Twisting

The next forming process is twisting. It is decorative and sometimes functional, as might be used to make skewers.

Cut off a 20-inch piece of 1/4-inch square mild steel. Draw out one end and form a loop as in the hook exercise. Use the cross peen of the hammer to close the loop of the handle.

Taper the other end and prepare to twist. Set the jaws of your vise to the size of the stock. Heat the piece, moving it back and forth through the fire to heat the bar over at least 12-inches. The bar will be hotter in the center and it is possible to make more twists in the center, because it is softer. This gives a graceful movement to the piece. Clamp one end of the piece in the vise. Do not clamp it where it is hot, since this mars the finish and breaks the even flow of the spiral. After the piece is in the vise, twist to form the spiral. Have a brush handy to clean off the scale on the spiral.

Twisting with a single twist and with a reverse twist..

To do a reverse twist, secure one end of the piece in the vise, and hold the handle firmly in one hand. With vise grips or pliers in your other hand, grip the metal in the center and twist. Do not allow the piece to turn in your hand as you are twisting it in the center. Be careful that the skewer does not wobble and get out of line. If it does, you can straighten it out later on the face of the anvil. The sharp edges of the spiral will be softened. A wooden mallet or brass hammer can be used without damaging the edges.

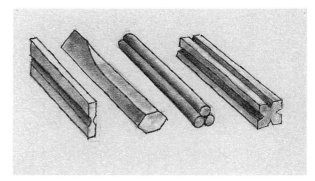

Sections to be twisted.

Skewers

Make a set of skewers with different handles and twists. When the set is complete wire brush them briskly and finish them with an edible oil, such as vegetable or olive oil. This type of oil can be carburized over the fire by heating the skewer and then reheating after applying the oil. This slightly burns the oil; it is the same darkening action that takes place on your pots and pans.

There are probably more twists that have been created by smiths that any other forging technique. Several basic types and section are shown for trials, but create your own!

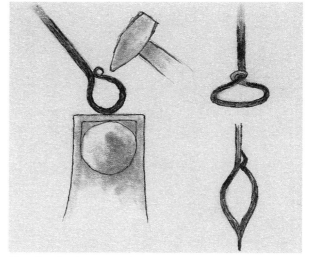

Handles for skewers and using the cross peen for shaping.

Fire Rake

Make a combination fire rake and poker with the techniques just described. This tool is handy for raking coal into the fire, breaking breeze and removing clinkers. Use 3/8-inch square stock 30-inches long. Form the handle first; this allows you to comfortably hold the piece and determine which way to bend the blade. With one of your newly created twists, twist the center section. Flatten the rake blade by bringing to an orange heat and laying it on the face of the anvil. Use heavy blows to spread the metal. Clean up the hammer marks and point the end. Bend the rake end for left or right hand use.

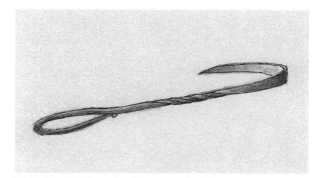

Right handed fire rake for use at the forge.

This project has a number of steps which are a little easier if done in the outlined sequence. Not all projects are this simple, and some require a great deal more study to determine the best sequence to do the forging and forming operations. Think in the fire.

Shutting Down the Fire

When you are shutting down for the day, you can let the fire just go out, but this wastes fuel. It is better to pull out the unburnt coke of the firebox, which is along the sides. Allow the remaining part of the fire to die out. To fire up again, dump the ashes and light up.

Now that the fire is taken care of, plan your work schedule for the following day. Do some drawings for the new pieces to be forged. Take some time to think about your movements and the efficiency of your layout.

Upsetting

Upsetting is the process of making a piece of steel thicker and is sometimes called "jumping up." It is the reverse of drawing out.

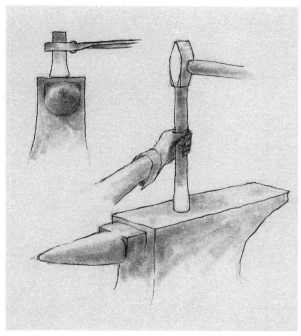

Upsetting on the anvil with tongs and hand held.

There are several ways to upset, depending on the size of the metal and its use. Upset short pieces on the face of the anvil. Hold the piece, hot end down, with tongs or gloved hand, and strike it on the cold end. In this way the heated part of the metal will be uniformly upset or thickened. (In contrast, when the heated end is struck with the hammer only the very end of the heated part is upset or spread. This is called "heading.")

When the end is gathered enough to hold, or catch, on the edge of the anvil, you can strike it with "backing-up blows." This gives you more control to finish upsetting the end and to shape it.

Upsetting on the anvil with backing-up blows.

Upset longer heavy pieces of steel against a heavy upsetting block or anvil placed on the floor. Ram the piece to be upset against the block; in this way, the combined weight of the piece and force of the smith upset the end. Cast iron blocks or anvils absorb the force and work well using this method because the metal does not bounce as much as it would from a steel mass.

Different effects in the upsetting process are illustrated: the metal is being upset normally in 1; in 2 the bends are out of line and must be straightened out before continuing to upset; 3 and 4 indicate the way in which an end curves under if the end is not flat; 5 shows a bar which is upset up the bar from the face, because the end was cooled before the bar was struck.

The end of the bar should be even and cut at right angles to the bar. Square up the end of the bar before you upset it. If the end is uneven, curves and bends form in the bar and you have to spend time straightening it. After each heat, straighten out the piece before you return it to the fire, not after you take it out of the fire.

Small Rope Hook

To make the hook, select a 1/2-inch round, mild steel rod and cut off a 12-inch piece on the cutoff hardie. (Or, you can roll the piece over the edge of a regular hardie as the piece is struck to cut the end evenly.) Bring the bar to a light yellow heat and upset the end. As you strike the bar, look at the end you are striking not the end to be upset. If you don't, you may miss the bar. In this case it is always good to work with gloves or hold the piece with vise grips. Work surely and quickly, since upsetting requires more heats than drawing out.

The force of your blows determines the shape of the upset. If you want to upset just the end, use light blows; if you want a longer length of upset, hit harder. Slightly chamfer the end if it is spreading too much. (Or, upset it on the step of the anvil by holding the bar at a 45° angle.)

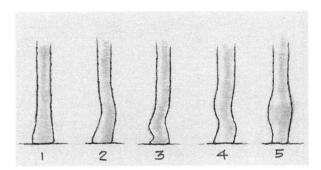

Different effects of upsetting a bar.

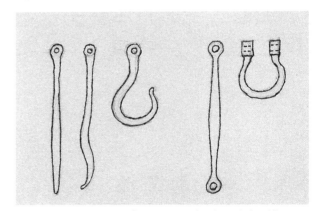

Layout of the steps to forge a rope hook and shackle.

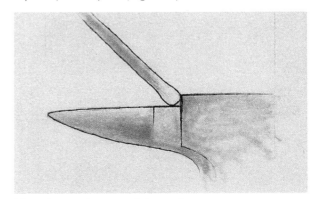

Upsetting on the step of the anvil.

46

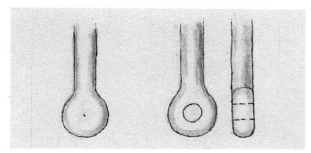

Upset and punched end of hook

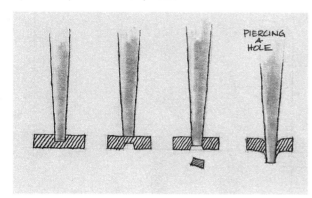

Steps in punching a hole.

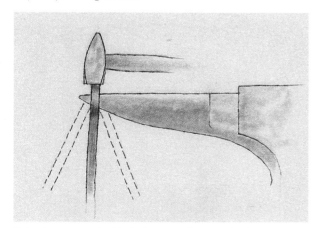

Enlarging a punched hole by spreading on the horn.

When the rod has increased in diameter to about 3/4-inch, form a ball on the end by holding the rod against the edge of the anvil and striking it with backing-up blows (or use the horn of the anvil). Bring the ball to a yellow heat and flatten it out until it is about a 1/2-inch thick.

Punch a 3/8-inch hole in the center. Bring the piece to a yellow heat and lay it down on the face of the anvil. Then drive the punch halfway through with four or five heavy blows. Quickly cool the punch. Turn the piece over, and place it over the center of the hardie hole. There is slight bulge on the side that has just been turned over, and the metal is slightly darkened at the point where it is being punched (because of cooling). As you hold the piece over the pritchel hole, place the punch on the bulge/dark spot and punch through. The slug falls cleanly through the hole. (In contrast, if you punch the piece from one side only, a ragged hole will result.) Shape this hole into an eye by using the beak of the anvil or a mandrel to enlarge the hole. Cut off the bar 8-inches from the eye and draw out the end. Shape the hook.

A shackle can be made in much the same way. Upset both ends, form a ball on each end; punch each to form an eye. Then bend the bar into a U shape.

The punching process can be done with many shapes and sizes. Make a 1/2-inch square punch. Practice punching a several holes 1-inch apart on a 1/4 x 1-inch bar, as below. Pre-measure and use a center punch to layout the centers. For a completely different effect, make a unique shaped punch and punch a series of holes in a bar.

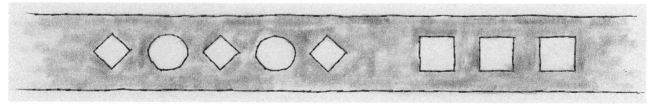

Spoon

To make a spoon use 1/2-inch mild steel, as you did for the rope hook, forming it in the same way, but finishing the end differently. Sketch several spoons before you begin work at the forge and plan your work.

1. Upset the spoon end and form a ball, which you will flatten later. The final shape is largely determined by the basic shape made at this stage.
2. Form the thin section of the handle where it joins the spoon.
3. Flatten out the spoon and shape the profile. While the iron is still hot, use an old file to shape the edges and make the spoon symmetrical.
4. Shape the handle, blending it into the spoon end.
5. Form the spoon. (See below.)
6. Finish with an edible oil. (Machine oils may have toxic additives.)

There are two ways to flatten out the end of the spoon. Heat the metal to a light yellow and strike it with hard flat blows. Either spread the metal with a cross peen hammer at right angles to the peen, or spread it uniformly in all directions with the face of the hammer. There are two ways to form the spoon using a ball peen hammer. The first is called peening. Heat the metal to a bright cherry and strike it with the ball peen on the face of the anvil and form a cup shape in the spoon. Begin striking in the center, and work gradually in a spiral till you reach the outer edge. Use lighter blows on the edge. The result is a peened surface. The second method is called sinking. Place the spoon over the punch hole or in a swage block and sink the metal into a circular form. Do not hit the metal too hard or it will stretch or buckle. You can make deeper forms more quickly this way. Whether you are peening or sinking, work in an even spiral with the hammer blows, beginning in the center and working out to the edge. This prevents distortion and creates an even shape.

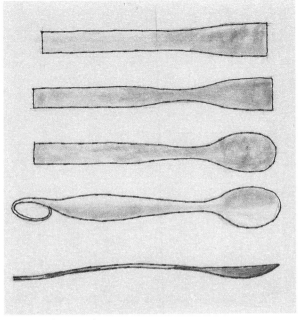

Steps in shaping the spoon.

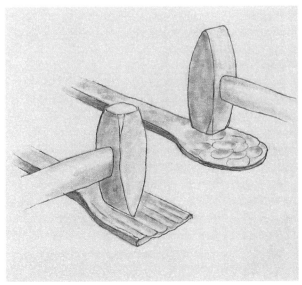

Flattening by using the peen and face of the hammer.

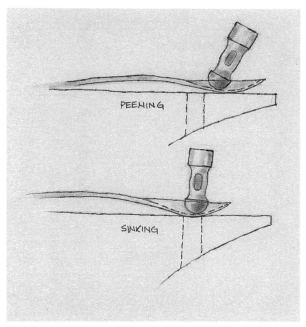

Developing the spoon form, which can also be done on a swage block.

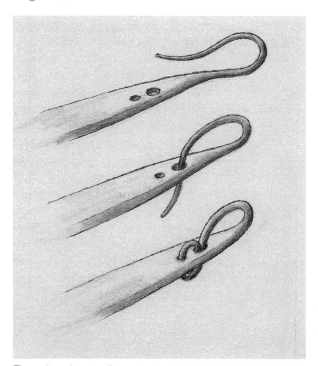

Threading the needle.

You can give final shape to the spoon when it is cold. If a great deal of cold work is to be done, the metal should be annealed. Anneal it by heating it to a cherry red and allow it to cool slowly in a dry medium like vermiculite. This removes the stresses in the iron and will allow it to be cold worked without the possibility of splitting the spoon.

There is another way to make a larger spoon or bowl from flats or sheet metal. Hammer the metal into a depression that has been carved in the end of a log or a block of wood. Use a ball peen hammer, forming hammer or wooden mallet to do this. Heat the portion of metal to be formed, place it over the depression and hammer it lightly. If you use a mallet with a rounded face, the bowl will be clear of hammer or peen marks.

Threading the Needle

Other ways to treat the handles for spoons, forks and spatulas are "threading the needle" and the spiral or "coil."

To thread the needle, draw out the handle end to a long thread of iron and punch a hole in the thick part of the handle. Holding the thread section with a pair of pliers, loop the end and thread it through the hole in the handle. Bend and twist the thread around the handle. You will probably have to take another heat since the thin sections cool rapidly. Round jaws pliers are the best for this job, because they do not mar the iron and make smooth bends.

The Spiral

The spiral is a joy to make because it grows as you make it and is transformed in the last step as you pull it.

Sketch out the steps with a soft aluminum or copper wire before you work with the hot iron. By sketching in wire first you are able to work various steps and you can determine the length of iron wire required.

Try it first with a piece of wire about 14-inches long and 1/16-inch in diameter. Clamp about 3 inches at the end of the piece in a vise. Bend the remainder at a right angle and quickly twist the wire counterclockwise (a). It is important to start properly. Remember that you must form both ends of the spiral in the same direction. You may have to reheat the wire several times as you make the spiral, because it tends to lose its heat rather quickly. Make about four complete twists, making sure that you close each turn tightly on the other (b); this ensures a round spiral.

Estimate the length of wire used to make the four twists, allow this much of the remaining wire to make another spiral and bend up the other end at a right angle (c). Heat this end and clamp it in the vise. Then form another identical twist, making sure to start your turn in the same direction. As the last turn is made, the two spirals lie on top of one another. Take an even light cherry heat, clamp one end in the vise, and with a pair of pliers, gently pull the other end (d). As you do this, the large turns pull out easily; the tight ones can be helped with a pick or screwdriver. You can close up or adjust the spiral by lightly tapping the coil with a hammer (e) as you gradually rotate it on the face of the anvil.

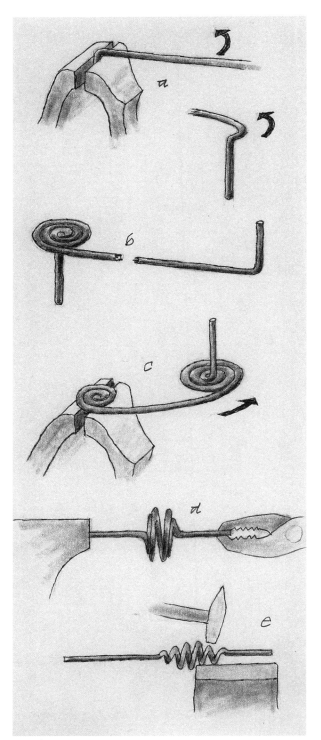

The spiral handle exercise.

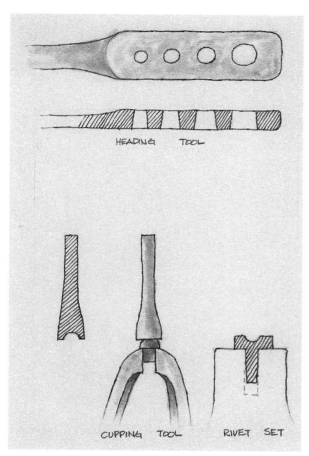

Heading and riveting tools.

Heading

Heading is used to make nails, bolts and rivets. To head a rivet, strike the heated end, with the result that only the end is upset.

Make a heading tool first. This is a strip of tool steel which has a number of round holes of varying sizes punched into it. These holes are tapered and are larger in diameter at the bottom, making it impossible for the piece to jam in the hole. To make this tool, form a strip of metal and punch holes in it. Taper them, from the back side, with a tapered punch or drift.

Then make a cupping tool. Grind a round point on the end of a bar that is 1/2-inch in diameter. This is the tool that will form the depression in end of the cupping tool. Grind it to the shape of the head of the rivet. Clamp it in the vise. Next, upset the end of another bar 1/2-inch in diameter. Drive this onto the tool. This is the cupping tool.

The rivet set is the bottom companion to the cupping tool. It prevents the end of the rivet opposite the head from being flattened when the rivet is in place and you are forming the top of the head. Make the rivet set with a shank so that it can be held in the vise or hardie hole. Use the same bar with rounded end to form the depression in the rivet set.

Make several rivets 1-inch long and 1/4-inch in diameter. Later you will need these for a pair of light tongs.

Select a 5/16-inch rod and draw out about 1-inch of the rod to a 1/4-inch diameter, using shouldering blows. Make it round. Rotate the rod over the cutting edge of the hardie and hit it with light blows. Do not cut it off; leave enough metal so that the rivet is still held on the rod. This allows you to place it in the fire without using tongs.

Bring the rivet to an orange heat and place it in the

heading tool. Break off the bar. Hit the top of the rivet quickly so that it spreads evenly and begin to form the head with the ball peen. After several blows, while there is still heat, use the cupping tool to shape the head. Then dip the header in water; the rivet will drop out, or can be lightly tapped out.

Do these things quickly to make the rivet in as few heats as possible. Think out the steps and then do them without wasted effort or motion. The time different smiths will be occupied over a given piece of work differs greatly. A smart smith will always do as much work as possible upon a forging in a single heat. While his iron is in the fire, he will mentally go through the sequence of operations and see that whatever is required is at hand, and when the iron is on the anvil he will strike quickly while the iron is hot.   [Paul N. Hasluck, *Smith's Work*, 1899]

Make up several more rivets and allow more material for the head. After shaping the rivet, reheat it and place it in the header. Create different decorative patterns on the head with chisels, punches and fullers. Decorative bolts can also be made from stock items. It is best to find bolts or rivets that are not plated with either zinc or cadmium, since heating these in the fire will cause toxic gases to be emitted.

Nails

Make a nail header with a square-tapered hole rather than a round hole, because a square nail is easier to make. Make the hole slightly smaller than the nail stock. Form the header with a raised shoulder. This makes it easier for you to head the nail with angled blows of the hammer.

Nails are made in basically the same way as rivets, but are usually made from thin square stock. First draw out a taper for the length of nail desired. Since the slightly thicker section is to be the head, nick it on a hardie just above the taper. Do not break it off. Take another heat and place the taper in the header and break it off. Finish off the head with the hammer. This is a good opportunity for

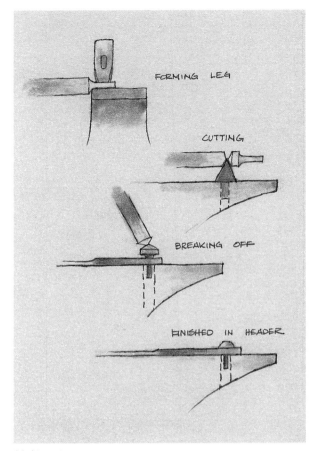

Making rivets.

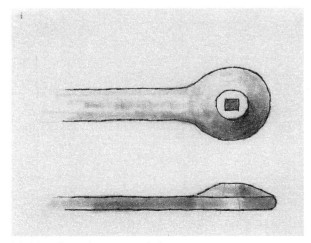

Nail header with a square hole.

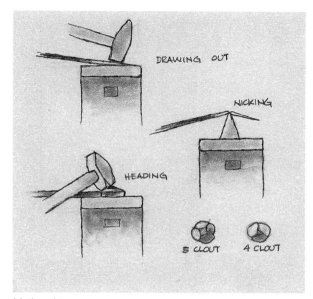

Nail making.

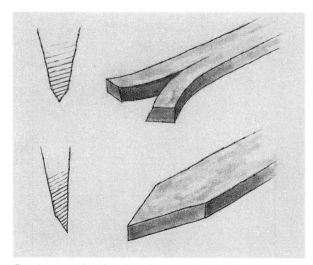

Chisel cuts with a bevel and a straight chisel.

you to try to develop a rhythm and pace in your work. Time yourself; see how long it takes to make 10 nails. Look at your work patterns and the way in which you handled your tools. Do 10 more nails. Time yourself. How can you increase your efficiency? How many rods do you have in the fire? How many nails can you make in an hour?

Upset rods of small diameter in the vise. Because they are thin, they have a tendency to bend if upset normally. Heat the rod, clamp it in the vise and strike it. The only disadvantage here is that the jaws of the vise make sharp corners on the rod as they grip it. This can be avoided if you use a spring header inside the vise to clamp the rod.

Splitting

Splitting is the process of cutting with a chisel. Hot and cold chisels make a beveled cut, but a cutoff chisel gives a straight cut. It is easier to work with a sharp chisel when you are making forks, spoons, spatulas and hinges.

Hinges

The butt hinge is named for the two pieces that mate or butt together and are joined by a pin. Make the hinge from a 1/8-inch by 2-inch or wider mild steel bar. Form the strap before you work on the eye. Practice splitting and the techniques that you have learned.

To start the eye of the hinge, bend a small section at the end of the piece down over the edge of the anvil. Turn the piece over and continue forming the eye with backing-up blows. Just before the eye closes upon itself, insert a piece of round stock (or a nail) into the eye, and continue rolling the eye around the pin. Tighten up the eye with the cross peen hammer. Form the eye for the other side of the hinge in the same way. To butt the hinges together, cut out the center section of one eye and the end sections of the other eye. Line up the hinges and mark both with a file where the cuts are to be made. Cut out a section in the middle of one of the pieces. Do this with a hacksaw, if the metal is cold, or with a chisel if the metal is hot. (Use a chisel with a flat side, so that it makes a vertical cut.) Cut the ends from the other piece. If you use a chisel to do all of the cutting, heat the piece to an orange heat with the pin in place, so that the chisel does not smash the eye. Keep the chisel cool by dipping it in water frequently. Then dress up the cut with a file to ensure that the two sections fit together properly. Place the pin through both eye sections to join them and cut the pin off allowing enough extra iron to form the head.

To head the pin, heat to an orange heat and quickly place it through the eyes of the hinge. Start to form the head, using a ball peen hammer and striking the pin with light, fast blows. The pin quickly lose its heat, so return the whole hinge to the fire, with the part that you are heading down in the fire. The headed part heats much more quickly than the rest of the hinge. You can finish it easily now. Rotate the hinge. If it is tight, return it to the fire, bring it to a cherry red and rotate it again to free it.

Split Tine Fork

Make a large fork by splitting; later we will make one by welding and compare the results. Make the split fork as follows:

1. Cut off a length of 1/2 x 1/4-inch stock.
2. Drill a 1/16-inch hole in the center of the tines which will prevent the metal from splitting. Take a heat split with a hot chisel down the center line.
3. Shape the neck and lower half of the handle.
4. Spread the tines and draw them out. Cut off the tines evenly after drawing out to the desired length. A saddle can be used to adjust the tines.
5. To complete this end, shape the tines and neck.
6. Shape the handle and hammer refine the sur-

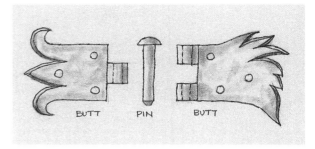
Parts of a hinge.

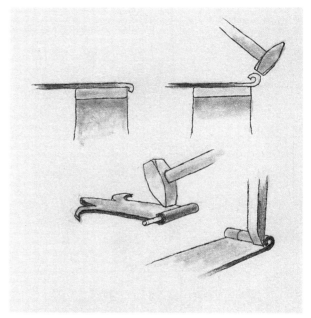
Forming the eye of the hinge.

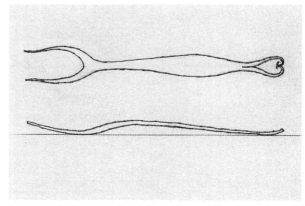
A top and side view of a fork with two different effects of splitting.

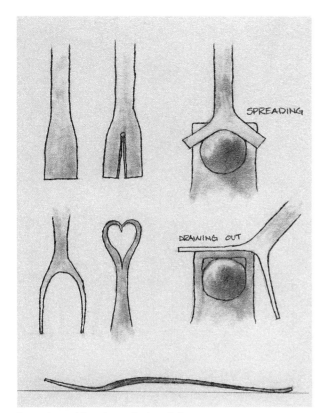

Steps in making the split tine fork.

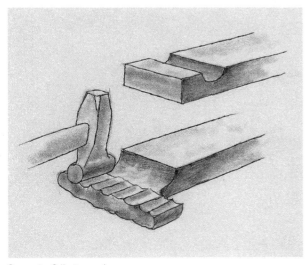

Steps in fullering a bar.

faces and any rough edges. Polish and finish the fork with a suitable oil.

7. Make a hook to hang the fork on.

When you are working with thin sections of metal, such as tines of a fork, be careful not to burn them. Turn the blast on only for a moment and watch the points carefully. Sometimes it is necessary to cool the points in the slack tub and return the fork to the fire to heat the heavier sections.

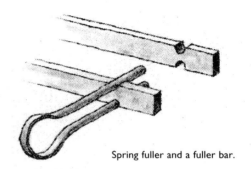

Spring fuller and a fuller bar.

Fullers

The fuller is a basic tool that is used to start many forming operations. It has a rounded nose that is either straight or curved. With it, you can notch or spread out the iron; in other words, you can change the cross section of the iron and change the direction of the metal.

A hand held fuller can be made in much the same way that you would make a chisel, except that you upset the end and then shape it to a round end.

A simple spring fuller is handy if you are working single handed. To make a spring fuller, cut off a 1/2-inch piece. of round stock, 36 inches long. Flatten out about 8 inches in the center of this piece until it is 1/4-inch thick. Bend this center section into a circle about 4 inches in diameter, and bring the ends of the piece together, forming jaws that are about 1 inch apart.

Trowel

Trowels, spatulas and garden spades and other bladed tools with a shank can be made in the following manner:

1. Notch a flat bar of metal with the spring fuller and then draw out this end to make a shank for insertion in the handle.

2. Make an offset bend in the shank. This is vital since it will be the guide for forming the center rib in the blade.

3. Make the blade of the trowel by gripping the shank with tongs and hold it upside down on the inner edge of the anvil. Flatten it on one side with heavy blows. Heat it again and flatten out the other side standing at the other end of the anvil. As you do this, a rib will form on the top of the blade. Continue to flatten and spread the blade. Trim the blade to the shape desired. Use a bench grinder or a file to shape the blade. Check for a uniform thickness of the blade.

4. Make a wooden handle and fit it to the shank. Drill a 1/4-inch lead hole in the handle; heat the shank and burn out the finished hole.

When the iron is first roughed down, its surface will not be smooth, though a good smith can impart a very fair finish to a flat surface by the hammer alone. The hammers should strike so as to bruise the work little as possible. There is a knack in using the hammer so that its edges will not mark the work, the blow being given by the central rounding portion of the face only. Striking fair with the middle of the hammer face, each mark serves to partly obliterate others, and leaves a very smooth surface, only slightly wavy. This is all a smith working single-handed can effect by way of finish. With the assistance of a hammerman the surface can be smoothed more effectually by means of a flatter, which is held with the right hand of the smith, and slid in turn all over the surface of the work while the hammer man strikes it with the sledge. Thus finished the work is left very smooth. [Paul N. Hasluck, *Smith's Work*]

This description by Hasluck aptly describes the technique for imparting a good surface on iron. Use it at the end of the third step above.

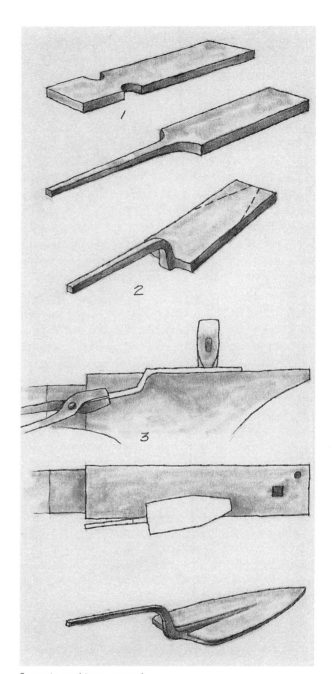

Steps in making a trowel.

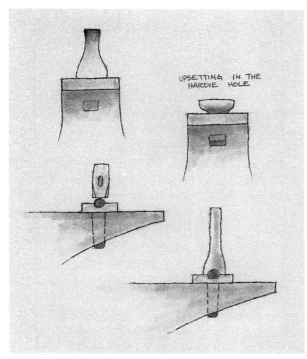

Upsetting a bar and making a swage for tenons.

Steps in making a tenon and shouldering it in a header.

Swages

A swage is used to give the metal its final form, after a piece of metal has been partially shaped with other tools. Swages are frequently used in matched pairs. Like the fullers, they can be spring mounted for the single-handed smith.

To make the bottom swage, use a short length of square bar which is the size of the hardie hole. Upset it to form a large end. Bring it to a yellow heat, place it in the hardie hole and flatten it out with a sledge. Form it into a rectangular block and square up the sides. Bring it to a yellow heat and place a 1/4-inch round rod over the center of the block. Hammer down the rod and make a groove in the swage that is one-half the depth of the rod.

To make the top swage, upset a bar to match the bottom tool. To make a groove in the top swage to correspond to the one in the bottom, prepare a 1/4-inch, U-shaped rod that will wrap around the heel of the anvil which will hold it in place. Place it in the groove of the bottom swage after bringing the face of the top swage to a yellow heat, place the top tool over the U, and hammer the swages together. This forms a groove in the top swage to match the one in the bottom swage. File off the inner edges of each swage so they do not pinch the metal. Temper the swages to blue if using tool steel. (See the section on Heat Treating Tools.)

This swage can be used more effectively to shape the leg of a rivet or a tenon rather than trying to make it round with a hammer.

Tenons

A tenon is a bolt-like extension at the end of a metal rod that serves as a connecting element. You can make a tenon with the swages just finished. Later this piece will be used to make a T-square to do layout work. Use a 1/2-inch square bar. Either place the bar on the edge of the anvil and draw out

57

the end with a hammer, or notch the piece with a small fuller (about 1/6-inch round nose, sometimes called a "viener"). A hardie can also be used, however, the disadvantage to using a hardie is it cuts rather that forming a radius and will weaken the leg of the tenon. Draw out the end to form the tenon. Heat to a yellow and place between the swages; strike them with a heavy hammer to shape the tenon. Then place the tenon in a 1/4-inch header and strike it to square the shoulder.

To make the T-square:
1. Use an 8-inch piece of 3/8-inch by 3/4-inch mild steel for the head.
2. Punch a 1/4-inch round hole in the center of this bar. Counter sink this hole and use chisel to make 4 deep chisel marks in the countersink. These chisel marks prevent the bar from rotating.
3. Cut the tenon 5/8-inch long with a hacksaw, and bring it to a light cherry.
4. Hold the main part of the T-square upright in a vise and place the tenon into the hole in the head piece. Strike the tenon with a light hammer using quick sharp blows. This will form a head on the tenon.
5. Square up your T-square with a carpenter's square, and peen the tenon till it is flush with the head.

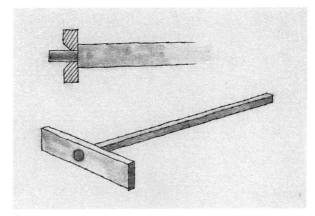

T-square with section drawing of counter sink on head.

When this type of tenon assembly cools, the part that was hot shrinks and pulls the assembly up tight. Heating the whole assembly will expand the parts and loosen them, so heat just the head of the tenon.

Monkey Tool

Another tool that can be used to form this shoulder on a tenon, it is called a "monkey tool." It is most frequently used on larger pieces that are too large to be moved or to be placed in a header or a vise. The tool is placed on the leg of the tenon and hammered to set the shoulder.

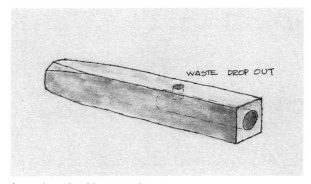

A monkey shouldering tool.

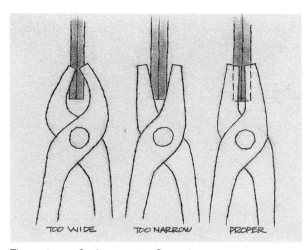

Three views of adjustments of tong jaws.

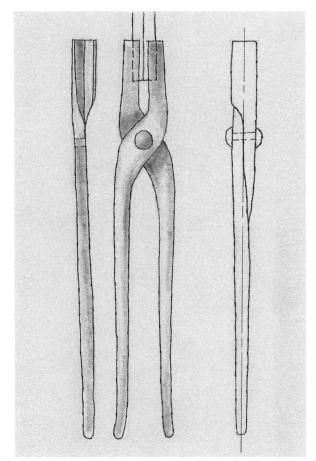

Views of tongs with a center line indicating the importance of the alignment to balance the pull on the reins of tongs.

Tongs

Tongs that are well made, that are easy to hold and that grip the iron well, make your work much easier at the forge. Good tongs last a long time and can be changed and reworked to do many jobs. Before each new job, adjust the jaws of the tongs so that they hold the stock properly. Then there is no danger of the hot iron slipping out of the jaws and you can work safely.

To adjust tongs, heat the jaws and hinge to a dull cherry. Place a small section of the piece of metal to be held by the tongs in the jaws. Clamp the jaws, holding the piece of stock in a vise and spread or close the reins as needed. Gently tap the rivet to close the jaws if there is any play in the reins. Open and close the reins to make certain that they are free to move. Notice how the tongs move more freely as they cool, the opposite of riveting the head of the tenon.

There are many uses for small tongs at the forge. Make several pairs, to get a feel for making tongs. These are easier to make than the heavy tongs explained later.

Study the detailed drawings of tongs and the steps involved in making them. These help you to visualize the way in which tongs are made and assembled. Note that both pieces of the tongs are exactly the same. Draw one side of the tongs and then trace it. Turn the tracing over and place it on the original drawing; as you do this, you see how the tongs mate and hinge.

Cut off two 12-inch lengths of 3/8-inch round mild steel. Upset one portion near the end of each piece (a). This is the hinge section and it should be heavier. Form the jaws and offset (b). Hold the handle at a 45° angle and turn the piece 90° to the left. Then flatten out the bulge section (c). Grade it into the handle. Turn the piece 90° again and form the S-curve of the tong (d). Shape and refine this curve by means of shouldering blows (e).

Draw out and taper the last one-third at the end of the reins. Make two identical pieces. Place them together and see how they match. If the pieces are slightly different, rework them and true up on a bending fork (f).

Place the two pieces together to determine where the rivet will connect them. Mark the spot with a center punch and then punch or drill a 1/4-inch hole in both pieces. You can place a 1/4-20 nut and bolt in the tongs to check out their movement. You should make any necessary adjustments now before riveting them together.

An alternate method of making the holes is to punch out the first hole. Heat the other tong and position it underneath. Quickly drop a little iron scale in the hole; the scale will leave a spot where the hole should be made.

Check the 1/4-inch rivets previously made for fit and length. The length of the leg of the rivet coming through should be slightly over twice the diameter of the rivet. Heat the rivet to a yellow heat and place it in the tongs. Then put the head of the rivet in the rivet set so that it is not be flattened. Strike your first blow of the top firmly and quickly with the face of a small ball peen hammer. This blow will slightly expand the entire length of the shank of the rivet to the diameter of the hole. Strike the next blows quickly; with the ball peen, head the end of the rivet by striking angled blows around the head of the rivet. When the head is roughly formed, take the cupping tool and dress up the rivet. This can be done in one heat with practice. If another heat is needed, put the tongs in the fire, bring them to a dull cherry red and finish the rivet. While still at a red heat, open and close them to allow the tongs and the rivet to conform to each other. Adjust the jaws and the reins to make sure they are aligned; the reins should be directly over one another, which prevents them from twisting in your hand when gripping. If the reigns are to tight, too close to one another, clamp

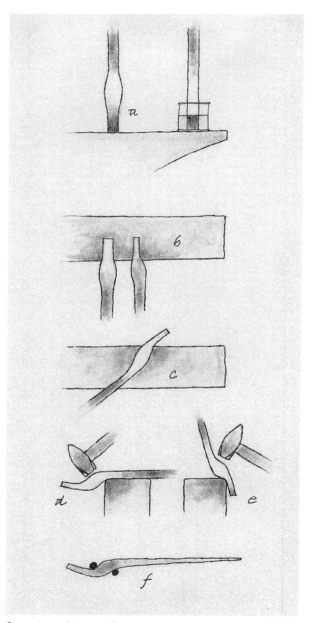

Steps in making small tongs.

60

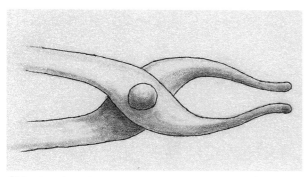

Pick up or bow tongs.

them in the jaws of a vise and pull the reigns apart.

You can also make a pair of bow pliers using this process. These are useful as pickup tongs. Make the jaws on these 2 to 3 inches long, round rather than square. The shape of the S curve in the throat should be more open than the other tongs. Prepare a drawing and use as a pattern for these tongs.

Welding

Successful blacksmithing depends on many techniques. An important one is forge welding. It is more difficult, because there are many aspects to keep in order and to do in proper sequence.

When ferrous metal is heated, it softens as the temperature increases and reaches the point at which two pieces of metal can be joined together by means of pressure or hammering. This a cohesive union is called "welding." The temperature at which this is possible is called the "fusion point," or a "welding heat." This temperature varies according to the alloying elements, particularly carbon.

Iron properly welded in the forge has no visible joints, because of the cohesive bond of the crystals of iron, this bond is the atomic bonding of the atoms of metal. It is not an adhesive joining, since there is no adhesive material joining the pieces. It is almost as strong (70%)as the parent pieces of metal, if properly heat treated.

Successful welding depends on the following: an understanding of the process, a knowledge of the material to be welded, the correct flux, a proper fire, preparation of the parts to be welded and the refinement of the grain after the weld has been made. It is necessary to add that forge welding is a dangerous activity. High heats bring on excessive amounts of ultraviolet and infrared radiation—use the proper safety equipment.

Flux

Wrought iron is the easiest of the ferrous metals to weld, because it is almost pure iron. Its welding temperature is very high and the scale melts before the welding heat is reached. As a result, no flux is needed. Steels with a small amount of carbon are easy to weld, and those with high carbon content are more difficult to weld. As the carbon content of the metal increases, the welding temperature decreases. At lower welding temperatures, the melting point of the scale will be too close to the welding temperature. This causes the scale to build up and form a barrier, rather than become fluid and flowing out of the weld area when struck. To prevent this, use a flux when you are welding high carbon steels. Flux serves two purposes: it combines with the scale and lowers the melting point and after the scale melts, it forms a protective liquid barrier over the iron, prevent further oxidation (scaling). Use flux sparingly for the following reasons:

1. If you use too much, it causes more scale formation rather than less, by attracting oxygen.

2. If there is too much flux in the weld, and it is not completely forced out by the first welding blows, it forms a barrier between the pieces to be welded.

Flux is not a glue. Welding is a process of cohesion, not one of adhesion. There are a few good commercial fluxes available, and in addition, there are many formulas for flux. The basic ingredients are clean sand and borax. Clean sand is a flux for mild carbon steels. When 4 parts sand and 1 part borax are used, the mixture becomes a general-purpose flux. Ordinary borax contains water, and when it is heated, it bubbles, melts and runs like water. After it cools, it is called borax glass (anhydrous). When this is pulverized and mixed 4 parts to 1 with sal ammoniac (ammonium chloride), the result is a good flux for carbon steels. Another flux for high carbon steels is 50% anhydrous borax, 25% boric acid and 25% silica sand. Crescent Weld and E-Z Weld are commercially available fluxes. Crescent Weld melts around

1700°F. to 1800°F. and E-Z Weld slightly higher.

E-Z Weld is 50% borax and 50% iron filings. Iron filings combined with flux serves two purposes: first as the iron approaches welding temperature, the iron filings will be burnt off first, preventing the pieces to be welded from oxidizing and secondly, when you hammer the pieces together, the remaining filings are forced out of the scarf faces, carrying away the dross, scale and flux.

A reducing fire is necessary for welding. It should be made up of a deep bed of coals and a cover of fuel over the pieces to be welded. (The cover helps to prevent oxidization.) Add more clean coke to the bed of coals before you put the piece in to start the welding heat. Heat the metal slowly in the fire to make sure that it is heated evenly. The blast should be low and steady; if necessary, the blast can be increased slightly just before removing the piece, to bring it up to welding heat.

Chambered Fire

There are several different types of fires for welding. The first one to use is a chambered fire. With this fire, you are able to look into the fire and examine the piece as it heats. Start the fire as you normally would and make plenty of coke. Use a lot of coal in building up the banks and pack it down hard. Fire bricks can also be used to build up a wall around the fire box. After the fire is well made, place a 3-inch piece of 2 x 4 on top of the coals. Turn on the blast, add more wet coal over the block and build up the pile to make a roof over it. It must be packed and wet down well. The coal soon cokes and forms a roof that supports itself. The wood burns away, leaving an opening in the front for putting in the iron. After you place the piece to be welded in the fire, you may want to cover the opening with a block of coke or a piece of sheet metal, since the full hot blast comes out of this opening. It helps to wear a glove, because this blast heats up the full length of the piece.

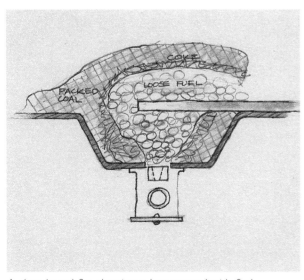

A chambered fire showing a bar covered with fuel.

Scarfing

Before welding two pieces of metal, you must shape them, so that they can be joined together properly. This is scarfing. The scarf is thicker than the rest of the piece, because the iron is thinned out when the pieces are hammered together. The convex shape of the scarf face is critical. When you hammer the two pieces together, the scale is forced out. The scarf faces must always touch in the center, not at the edges. (Flat pieces and bars are easier to weld than round pieces; rounds have a tendency to slide off one another when they are struck.)

Our first weld is an eye weld. Make the scarf on an 18-inch bar of 1/2-inch by 3/8-inch mild steel. Upset the end so that it is 1 1/2 times the size of the stock, and then form the scarf using backing-up blows. The face should be convex and the end should come to a blunt point with a thin edge. Now bend the loop to form the eye at the end of the bar.

Place it in the chamber of the fire and bring it to an orange heat. Remove it from the fire and quickly sprinkle on the flux. Return it immediately to the fire. (At an orange heat, scale flakes away from the iron, allowing the flux to combine easily with the newly formed scale. At a cherry red heat, the scale adheres tightly to the iron and forms a barrier. Therefore always add flux at an orange heat to get the maximum benefit of the flux.) Flux can also be added to the pieces to be welded in the fire; use a long handled spoon to add the flux directly to the parts.

Turn on a low blast, making certain that the weld area is in the center of the fire. You may have to push the piece through the fire to locate it properly. When the piece reaches a light yellow heat, turn it over so that the weld faces down in the fire. Be careful to keep the weld area clean.

As the piece approaches welding heat, the flux will

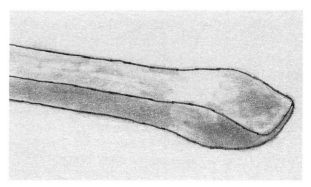

Scarf face.

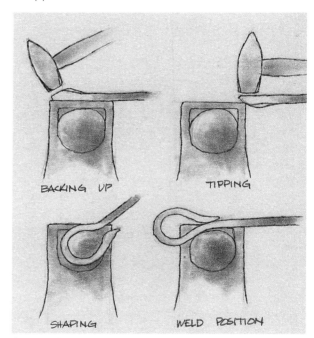

BACKING UP

TIPPING

SHAPING

WELD POSITION

Steps in forging the scarf and making an eye weld.

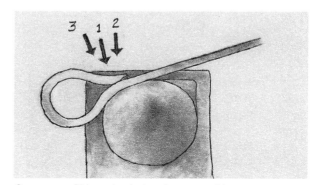

3 1 2

Sequence of blows in closing the eye weld.

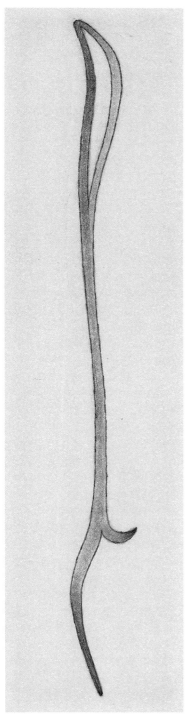

Poker with two loop welds with one cut open and drawn out.

flow and form a smooth protective coating over the weld area. The iron comes to welding heat shortly after this, and the piece is a light yellow. (It is bright and difficult to look at.) The surface has a greasy or glassy appearance. When a few sparks start to come from the fire, it is at welding heat!

Your eyes may adjust to the bright light of the welding fire or you may be momentarily blinded when you shift your attention to the anvil. Don't stare directly into the fire for long periods of time, for this reason. Blink your eyes frequently. You can try sunglasses for the first welds; they cut down the blinding glare and enable you to see the fire more easily. But you must wear safety glasses, because of the high levels of radiation and the cascade of sparks when the weld is struck. *An absolute must!* My two pair are "Thermonon"and didymium lens with shields on the sides.

The anvil should be clean of scale. Place the hammer on the anvil ready to pick up. When the piece comes out of the fire, you should know exactly what you are going to do, and it should be done without hesitation. Don't forget, think in the fire and don't waste time, because the piece is cooling quickly. Don't stop and look at the piece. Strike it!

When removing the piece from the fire and as you are moving to the anvil, flick the piece like a paintbrush. (Or, you can gently tap the piece on the side of the anvil.) This throws off any dirt or coke which might be around the weld. Place the piece on the anvil and strike the blows as numbered. The first blows to close the weld should be light and quick, then gradually make them heavier. Generally it is better to use a lighter rather than a heavier hammer. Turn the piece on its side and work the sides. When the piece cools to an orange heat, wire brush each side quickly then sprinkle on some more flux and return it to the fire. Bring it to a welding heat. Finish off the weld by continuing to work the sides and blending the eye with the stock. One or two more welding heats should be enough to finish the weld. Finishing the weld area means closing the lines that are formed when the two pieces come together, called "cold shuts." The wire brush is most important with this task; use it frequently to clean the area and flux before returning to the fire.

Welding greatly enlarges the grain size of the metal and therefore weakens it. When you are shaping the eye, continue hammering over the entire weld area until the piece cools to a dark red. Use light finishing blows. This is called "hammer refining." This technique reduces the size of the grain and restores the metal's original strength. Make a weld on the other end of the bar, making the eye 1 1/2-inches in diameter.

If the welds do not hold, examine the weld areas. If the eye was partially welded, only part of the weld was at welding heat. If there are dark spots in the weld area, there was dirt or flux in the weld, or the fire was oxidizing, forming excess scale preventing cohesion. If the metal is pitted and has a mottled look, it is burned. Cut it off and start again, being more careful this time.

Fire Poker

Make a fire poker with the piece that has just been welded. Cut one loop with a chisel and shape the poker end to a point. Then form the hook end over the beak of the anvil. Shape and finish the poker halfway up the handle, cool it and work on the handle end.

Cut the blast; examine the bed of coals. The level of coals is considerably lower, because the fire has burned a good bit of fuel for the welding heat. Look for clinkers and remove them, rotate the tumbler or grate, and dump the ash. After cleaning the fire and add more fuel. You can add hard coke or breeze to this fire now. The metallurgical coke is useful for welding because it burns long and clean.

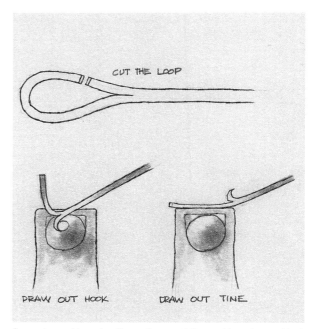

Steps in making the fire poker and for making the welded tine fork.

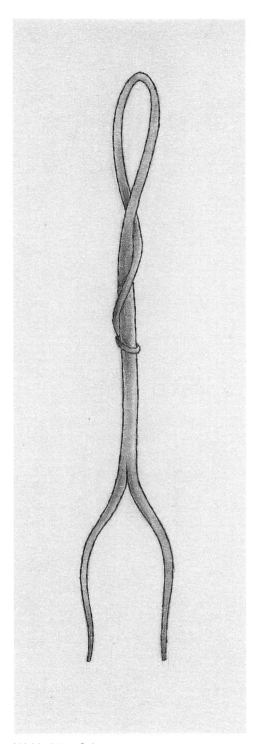

Welded tine fork.

Open Fire

There is another type of fire that can be used for welding. It is called an open fire. After you clean the fire, break up the top (the roof of coke), and allow it to burn, while you build up the sides of the fire and pack them down again. Break the breeze into small pieces so that the work can be moved easily through the fire. It takes more experience to weld with this type of fire, but after a while, you will find it is also a good fire. This is because the metal is completely surrounded by fuel and is protected from scaling. Flux can also be added directly to the pieces in this type of fire. Make a long handled spoon for this purpose.

Welded Tine Fork

Cut off an 18-inch piece of 3/8 or 1/4-inch square mild steel rod to make a welded barbecue fork. One end will be a loop for hanging and the other end will be cut apart to form the tines. Scarf the ends and make loop welds on each end. If you are working in an open fire, gently lift the piece to see if it is at welding temperature. Do not move it around more than necessary or you get dirt in the weld area. Another indication that a welding temperature has been reached is the start of sparks coming from the fire. The sparks appear sooner if you are using a flux that contains iron filings, so judge the welding temperature by the surface appearance of the steel.

Cut the larger eye in half and draw out the tines. Then straighten and smooth them on the face of the anvil. Bend the tines over the beak. Compare the welded fork with the split fork. By comparing different techniques and evaluating their merits you will be able to select the method which is best suited to the needs of the task. It is an important aspect in designing wrought iron pieces because each method will give slightly different results.

Faggot Weld

It is sometimes difficult to get a feel for all of the variables in welding. Experiment with the faggot weld to help to improve this touch. This weld will bring a mass of steel to the end of a bar more quickly than upsetting it would. Bend over 2 inches of a 1/4 x 1/2-inch bar and double it back. Place it in the fire and bring it to an orange heat. Sprinkle flux on each side of the weld and return it to the fire. Bring to welding heat, fling away the dross and make the weld.

Try another faggot weld, but scarf the end and compare the welded area. The line that you see on the weld done without the scarfed end is called a "cold shut." This will make the piece weaker at that point.

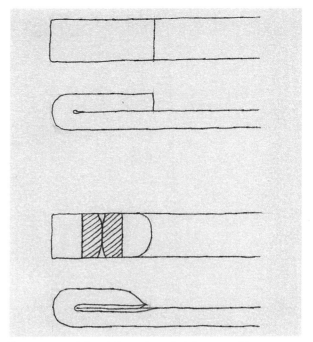

Bars prepared for plain and scarfed faggot welds.

Large Tongs

The size of the tongs that you can make by the previous method is limited because you have to upset the joint area and draw out the long section of the reins. You can make larger tongs using a lap weld, which is an overlap of two pieces usually of different sizes. If you have a helper (a striker), you can make the tongs more quickly.

To make a pair of flat jawed tongs use 7/8-inch square mild steel. You will need about 4 to 5 inches for each jaw. They may be made from separate pieces or from opposite ends of the same bar.

First, fuller notches about 3/8-inch deep on the top and bottom of the bar with a top fuller. At a 45° angle, fuller another notch on the side that intersects with the top notch. Flatten the jaws and then spread the hinge area at a right angle to them. Be careful to preserve the fillets formed by the fuller, so that the jaws are not weakened by sharp corners. Refine the shape of the jaws and form the inset or notch in the jaw with a square bar. This inset holds both square and round pieces firmly.

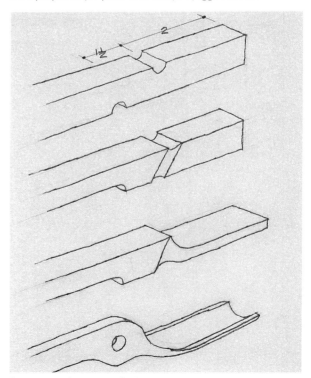

Steps in making jaws for large tongs.

Punch a 3/8-inch hole for the rivet. Then cut off the piece about 3 inches from the hole. Form a scarf for welding on the reins.

Lap Weld

Make the reins from a rod which is 14 to 15 inches long and 1/2-inch in diameter. Prepare the rods for welding. But before you weld the tongs, practice with scrap stock. Cut off two pieces long enough to heat without tongs. Upset the ends and make the scarfs, either with the edge of the anvil or with the cross peen. The scarf must be convex, formed at a 45° angle, and drawn to a point. The slight return on the end of the scarf will stay hot when the two are joined for welding.

As mentioned previously, the fire must be a reducing fire that is clean and hot. Clean the fire out and prepare a deep well-banked fire. Clean off scale from the face of the anvil. Place a medium-weight hammer on the face of the anvil where you can grasp it quickly. Plan your movements from the fire to the anvil and the way in which you will lay the pieces down on the face.

Place both pieces in the fire scarf down, so that no dirt lodges there. Bring to a light orange heat and add flux. Make certain that each piece in the fire is heating evenly. Pull one back if it heats too fast; usually it will be the thinner piece. Don't allow the pieces to touch, as they might stick together in the fire. When they have reached welding heat, come away from the fire and gently tap both bars, scarfs down, on the outer edge of the anvil in order to dislodge dirt. Place them quickly in position for welding. Hold the left piece scarf down and on top of the other piece to hold it down. Let go of the right-hand piece with your tongs (let the tongs drop to the floor) and grab the hammer. Strike the first blows immediately. They should be light, for heavy blows might knock the pieces out of alignment. Strike the second or third blow on the lip of the scarf to weld it. Turn the piece and close the other lip. Now strike increasingly heavier blows to

Placement of scarfs and striking order to complete a lap weld.

close the weld and shape it. When the piece is at an orange heat, wire brush all scale off and quickly sprinkle a little flux on the weld line. Return it to the fire. Bring the piece to a welding heat and finish closing the weld by working around the weld lines. One or two heats should complete the weld.

Practice this sequence of welding several times before trying to weld the tongs. The important sequence with this weld is to make the placement of the pieces and then drop the tongs used to hold the jaws. Since this is the heavier part it should be the one to be on the face of the anvil. It will hold more heat and is less likely to cool before the weld has been closed.

If you are satisfied, try welding the reins and jaws of the tongs. Notice that the jaws are heavier and will take longer to heat. Watch the color of the pieces in the fire carefully. Hold the jaws with tongs in your right hand and the reins in your left hand. When you place the scarfs together, they will stick together if the proper welding heat has been attained. Hammer refine the weld areas above a cherry red and continue until a dark red heat. This brings the tongs to an optimum strength. Assemble the reins together with a 3/8-inch rivet and adjust the tongs.

Other Welds

To gain experience, try some different types of welds, such as the butt weld, the jump weld, T and angle welds and the cleft weld. To make a butt weld, heat two bars of similar size to welding heat and butt them together by hammering the ends together. They upset one another as this is done (a). Finish the weld by hammering the sides; use a top and bottom swage to true up the shape. In general, use the butt weld on heavy pieces (3/4 inch and over) and the lap weld (described earlier) for thinner sections of metal.

The jump weld (b) joins a bar to a plate or anoth-

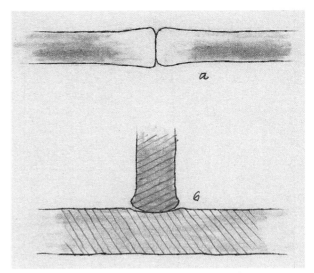

A butt weld and a section through a jump weld.

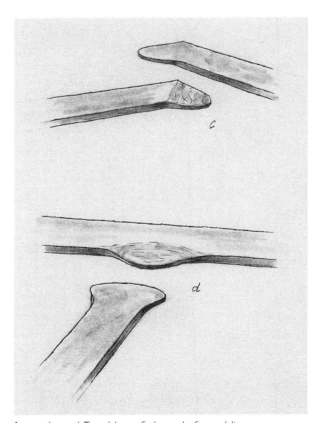

An angle and T weld scarfed, ready for welding.

70

er bar. This weld is sometimes used to make bottom swages and other anvil tools. Prepare the two pieces to be joined; form a convex scarf on one end of the bar and a concave scarf at the center of the plate. When you weld these together, the center of the convex scarf on the bar must touch first to force out any scale, dirt or flux that is present (b). This is critical. After the stem is welded to the plate, turn it upside down and put it in the hardie hole. Hammer it in which sets the stem.

Scarfs for an angle weld are mirror images of one another (c). Upset the ends and develop the scarf, making sure that the edge is no thinner than a 1/16-inch; if it is, it tends to burn and to cool quickly. When you place the pieces on the anvil to weld them, place them together as you do when you are making a lap weld, but at a right angle to one another.

Make the T weld (d) in much the same way. Upset the end of the T and the place in the bar where it will be welded. Make each scarf face convex. (When you upset pieces to be welded, make them half again as thick as the original piece.) When you make an angle or T weld, close the weld with two or three blows. Quickly turn the piece to work the other side. Then return it to the fire and finish the weld.

With the cleft or V weld, spring steel can be welded to mild steel; this is called "steeling." (This is used when the combination of tough steel and hard steel are required, as for chisels, axes and froes.) Form the lips of the cleft to wrap around the end of the piece of spring steel. This cleft grips and protects the spring steel in the welding fire. (Use a flux containing 1 part sal ammoniac and 4 parts borax.) Remember, when you are welding steels with two different carbon contents, their welding heats are different. Place the mild steel in the fire to get maximum heat; push the spring steel through the fire to protect it. As the mild steel approaches welding heat, pull the cleft to the

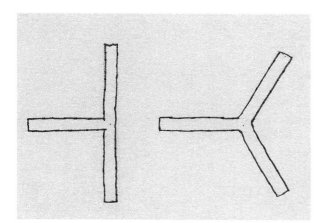

A "T" weld opened to an equal angle assembly for legs

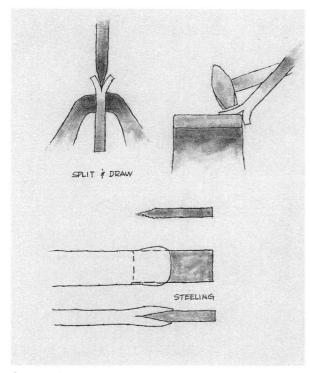

SPLIT & DRAW

STEELING

Steps in the steeling a tool steel blade on a mild steel bar.

center of the fire for the final heat. Make the weld and finish off the part as necessary.

Welding Tips

Welding iron is a series of critical operations. It is not difficult, if you keep all of the elements under control. Make sure that you have scarfed the pieces properly, that the fire is a reducing fire, that you remove the piece from the fire at the proper time, that you have positioned the pieces properly and that you strike them quickly and surely.

Many people are completely befuddled by welding. However, when you have done each step carefully, and have "closed" a weld, you feel more confident. Your first weld may be the hardest, but as you learn and gain confidence from each successful weld, each one that you do will be easier.

Look at the iron in the fire. When you are welding mild steel, it is at a welding heat when the color of the metal and the color of the fire are one and the same: a light, bright yellow. In contrast, tool steel at welding heat is a shade darker than the color of the fire. Learn to judge these things through experience.

Remember, "fire welding" is bringing two heated pieces of metal together at the proper temperature to cohesively bond together by hammering. To achieve this bond the welding temperature is critical. If the weld is too low the pieces will not bond; if the weld is too high there is danger of it burning and not welding because of excessive oxidation.

There is another way to test for welding heat. Place a piece of iron in the fire. Take a small rod, a 1/4-inch in diameter, that has been drawn to a dull point. As the piece to be welded approaches welding heat, place the rod in the fire. Use the rod to check for welding heat. As the piece approaches the welding heat, it will be soft and slippery. Sometimes the pieces will stick together. Try this test; it is very useful in helping you to see the welding colors. As the iron heats up to this temperature it is called a "slippery welding heat." As the temperature increases further it is called a full "welding heat."

I have found that you must pay strict attention to your work when you are welding, perhaps more than at any other time. If you allow your thoughts to wander, you might burn the metal or miss the moment when welding heat has been reached. When welding heat has been reached, the metal "speaks" to you; it gives off sparks, saying, "weld me."

Chain

Chain links are made with a lap weld. Cut off some pieces, 7 inches long and 3/8-inch in diameter (one length per link). Take one piece and bend it into a U shape, making sure that the legs are 3/4-inch apart. If it is uneven, equalize the legs of the link by putting it in the swage block and hitting the long end. Then scarf the ends by holding it flat and at a 45° angle to the step of the anvil. Strike successive blows on its end, as you move it to the left toward the horn. Turn the U over and do the other leg. Do not make the scarfs less than 1/6-inch thick on the end or they will be too thin to hold a welding heat. Close the end by bringing the scarfs together. Bend the legs at an angle; do not try to round the corners yet. This bend will concentrate the heat at the scarfs when you put the link in the fire to bring the ends to welding heat. It is also be easier for you to hammer the weld.

Bring the link to welding heat and close the weld on the face of the anvil. Strike several light blows on each side and then place the link on the horn of the anvil to finish the weld. If necessary take another heat and give the link its final shape on the horn of the anvil.

Prepare the second link and complete the weld. Make a third and loop the other two onto it. Then

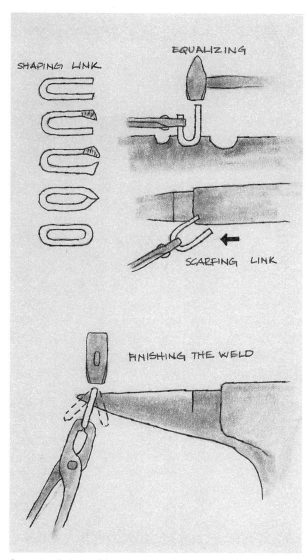

Steps in chain making.

weld the third link. You can add successive links one by one as you make them, or make several groups of three and then weld them together.

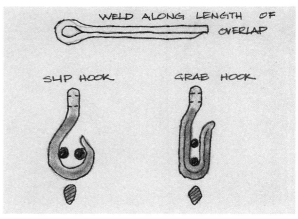

Welded bar hooks.

Slip and Grab Hooks

Make a welded slip hook and grab hook by bending a length of steel double and forming an eye at the looped end. Weld the overlapped portion and shape this part into the hook. Don't forget to hammer refine the weld area when finishing the hooks. Because these hooks and the chain links are welded, "normalize" them after forging to relieve the welding stresses. Normalizing is bringing the parts slowly up to the critical temperature and allowing them to cool slowly.

Making a Ring

Small rings made of 3/8-inch round or smaller can be made similar to chain. Rings of thicker section or flats should be upset on the ends first. This is needed to compensate for loss of metal due to welding.

To make a ring of 3/8 x 3/4-inch bar determine the inside diameter of the ring and calculate the circumference. To this (the length of the bar) add 1 1/8-inch, three times the thickness of the metal, to account for an upsetting and the overlap of the scarfs on each end. Upset each end and form scarfs making certain to have the scarfs face one another when the bar is bent into a circle. Form the circle and position the scarfs with a 1/2-inch overlap. Practice how the ring is to be brought to the horn of the anvil; this can be tricky on small rings since you have to bend down to place the ring in the proper position. Be careful since this position brings your face close to the weld. (If the ring is large then it can be worked on the face of the anvil.) Bring to a welding heat and set the weld. True up the ring over a cone mandrel. Check the diameter of the circle and make as necessary.

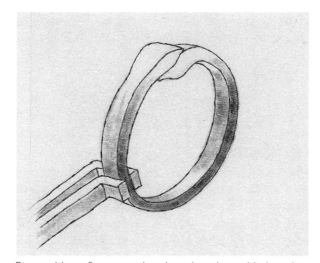

Ring weld scarfs prepared and ready to be welded on the horn of the anvil with offset tongs holding the ring.

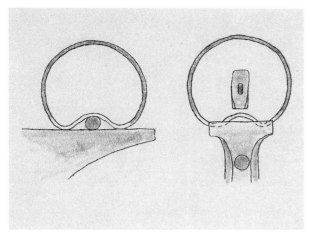

Shrinking a ring by upsetting a portion of the ring.

Upsetting a Ring

You may occasionally want to make a ring or hoop smaller. It may be a ring that has stretched, or it may be one that was too large to begin with. If you upset a portion of the ring, you decrease the circumference and, of course, the diameter.

Heat the ring and place it over a round bar on the anvil. Using a hammer, form a hump in that section of the ring. Heat it again and clamp it in a vise. Upset the hump by hammering directly on it. Then reform the ring into a circle. The area that has been upset is thicker, but the ring is smaller in diameter.

Decorative Iron

The history of wrought iron is replete with wonderful examples of decorative wrought iron. The iron examples in the "Edges of the Anvil" represent the varied dimensions of yesterday's metalworkers and of today's artist/blacksmiths. Use them all as models to experiment. In all of these exercises explore new directions, invent, create and experiment. By no means let this book or any other book dictate the direction in which you take your iron work. These exercises are meant to show how to do it and hopefully to open doors.

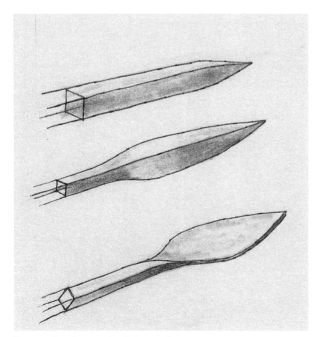

Steps of making a leaf from a bar.

Simple Leaves

In the decorative aspects of wrought iron, smiths have used a incredible variety of twists, geometric forms, animals and natural motifs. One form that is used universally is the leaf.

To make a leaf, select a 3/8-inch square bar and point the end; 2 inches from the end fuller out a 4-inch square section on the horn, to form the branch. Flatten out the pointed end on the diamond. This forms the basis of the leaf and stem. With a cross peen hammer, peen in ridges to give the effect of veins, waves and patterns on the leaf.

Try this with different sized squares and rounds. Notice that the shape of the part before it is flattened determines the shape of the leaf. Design your own or use nature as a model.

Collars

Ornamental ironwork is frequently assembled by means of collars. Occasionally they are called "bands." Gates, railings, signs, grilles and many household accessories fall into this category of assembly.

Scarf Collar

To make a scarf collar or band, first, make a mandrel by doubling over the stock that has been used to make the scrolls. Bend the collars around this, while the metal is hot. Determine the collar length by rolling the mandrel over the stock used to make the collar. (This stock should be smaller than the stock for the scroll.) Using a chisel or hardie, make a diagonal cut partially through the metal, at the places you have marked off for each collar. Heat the bar and form the collar, then snap off the partially formed collar. Then complete the collar. While the collar is still hot, open it up with a pair of pliers, so that you can place it around the scrolls. After all the collars are formed, place several of them in the fire on a wire hook, or use a pair of pickup tongs with a coupler on the reins. In this way, they will not be lost in the coals. When they reach an orange heat, place the collar around the scroll. Close it with a small hammer, then use pliers to squeeze the scarfed ends together.

Overlap Collar

To determine the length of an overlap collar, add the circumference of the pieces to be joined to a figure which is 2 1/2 times the thickness of the collar. Cut off a piece for one collar and draw each end to a thin taper. Then cold-form the collar into a U-shape. Clamp it in a vise over a mandrel made of the pieces to be joined. Make the first bend so

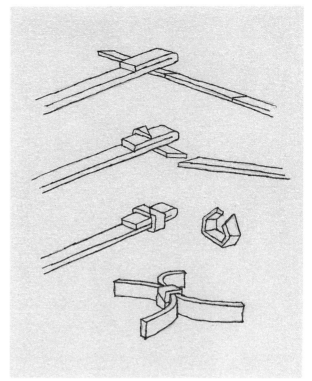

Forming and closing a scarf collar.

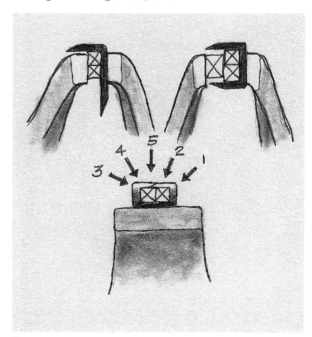

Steps in making an overlap band.

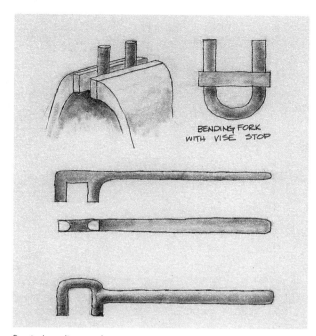

Basic bending tools.

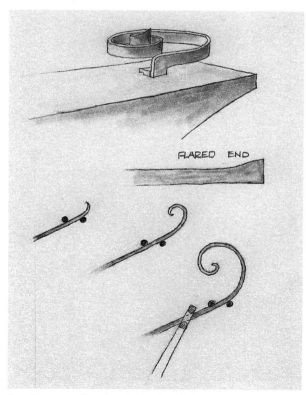

Bending a scroll tool with bending forks.

that each leg of the U will be equal. Make the second bend around a mandrel and a spacer. To install the collar, heat it and put it under the scrolls. Form the first leg over with angled blows. Then form the other leg over the first to overlap them. (A side blow tends to open up the collar, whereas the angled blow will tighten it.) Because of the overlapping ends of this collar, it is stronger than the scarfed band and has a finished look.

Bending Tools

Make the bending tools to use for decorative pieces. As with most blacksmithing tools, you will soon find many other uses for them at the forge.

There are two types of bending forks: those held in a vise and those placed in the hardie hole. The simplest ones are held in the vise; these are U-shaped forks. Select 1/2-inch and 3/8-inch round stock and make several forks of different sizes, varying the distance between the tines. Form the tines after you finish the welding.

Scroll or bending wrenches are hand held bending tools. Use them in scrolling, bending or straightening.

Scrolls

Scrolls are the filigree of the king's court. If your interests lie in the decorative area, the uses of scrolls are limitless. Although a scroll can be made free-form on the anvil, you will soon find that the scroll tool is a great help. Since scrolls are almost always used in multiples, the scroll tool enables one to make uniform scrolls quickly.

To make a scroll tool, draw the outline of the curve and trace it onto a piece of sheet metal. When you are making the scroll tool, the hot metal can be checked on this pattern. Flatten the end of a 1/4 x 3/4-inch bar and flair it up. (Use this flared end to start the scroll.) Then develop the curve of the scroll on the anvil. After you have made two complete revolutions in the development of the curve, bend the end of the tool at a right angle and double up the end to fit the hardie hole. Form the shank so that the scroll is about 1-inch off the face of the anvil.

Rectangular bars are generally used to make scrolls, although scrolls can also be made from round or square bars. To make the scroll, first finish the end of a 1/8-inch by 1/2-inch by 24-inch strap and start the scroll on the edge of the anvil or the scroll tool (a). Then heat at least 12 inches of the strap before bending the scroll. Place the end of the scroll on the raised tip of the scroll tool and grip them together with a pair of round-nose pliers. Then bend the strap in the direction of the curve. When one turn is complete, the scroll will drop completely into the tool. If enough of the bar is at a good heat, you can complete the bending in one heat. If the bar has cooled, return it to the fire and heat the portion to be bent.

Make the two basic scrolls, the C and the S in this tool. To make the S, turn the metal over to make a reverse curve. Make a number of different scrolls and it is easy to lay them out to design different patterns.

Trivet

Make a trivet to get the feel of making scrolls and assembling them. On a piece of paper, trace out a grouping of C-scrolls to see how they would fit together. Then cut the stock into equal lengths and make the scrolls. To assemble the pieces, make enough collars to join the scrolls together. Plan for extra collars on the outside of the scrolls to bring the piece to the same level; these collars could be wider and decorated by incising before forming. Allow extras for practice.

When this type of trivet is assembled, the pieces can be wired together and then place on one collar at a time. It is also common practice to tack weld the scrolls together where collars will placed. If an

COOL THE END TO GRAB THE SCROLL TOOL

Using the anvil and a scroll tool for forging the ends.

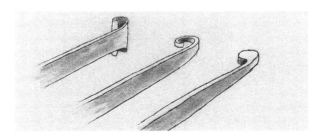

Different scroll ends.

C- and S-scrolls and a trivet.

78

assembly is to be riveted use small bolts to tie the piece together.

Polishing

Forged iron has a truly remarkable quality when polished. Polishing is the mechanical abrasion of the surface to highlight the iron and to reveal the hammered and formed surfaces. This aspect, more than any other, brings out the surface quality of the iron. The high spots are bright and the lower areas are dark revealing the surface texture. Try different methods of polishing on the leaves and in the following exercises. Allow for extra time since this polishing takes more time than you might estimate.

Various grades of emery or abrasive cloth work well. Abrasive paper has a tendency to crack and break apart easily and is more difficult to use. On larger pieces courser grades can be used, 80 grit; on smaller delicate pieces use a finer grade, 120 grit. 3M makes a tough nylon impregnated pad, "Scotch Brite," which comes in three grades: fine, medium and coarse. Wheels for power equipment of this material are available, which are great for simple flat pieces without protrusions. But, you must be extremely careful with this on a power wheel. Any part that has elements for the wheel to grab will be sent flying around the shop. Wire wheels can also be used, however they do not remove as much scale and do not polish the base metal in the same way. Another danger is that the wire elements in the wheel have a tendency to leave home and stick in your chest.

After polishing a part, clean it with kerosene or mineral spirits to remove any dirt and loose scale. The kerosene or mineral spirits also coats the metal with a light oil and helps to keep it from rusting. Later wipe down with a dry cloth prior to applying a protective coating.

Polishing is one of the subtle aspects to metalworking that brings life to metal. Bring it to life.

Fitting and Assembly

For the trivet, a little planning was needed to assemble it. On large, more complex projects where there are more parts and pieces to be fitted together, considerable time and effort will be required. It is an area that requires skill, experience and patience. Most smiths, when they attempt their first large job, fail to anticipate the amount of time involved in fitting and assembly. To help in understanding these aspects try keeping a time log of your various tasks, and a clearer time picture will form. Try this with the table described below.

Small Table

From the drawing, make a full size drawing of the table you are going to fabricate. Change the proportions, material sizes and dimensions to suit your design; decorate the edges and frame if desired.

Forge the legs from 1/2-inch square stock. Upset the end of each leg slightly, which will give the effect of each end having a foot. Develop a tenon on the top of each leg 1/4-inch diameter 1/4-inch long. Create three fullered lines around each leg with a 3/8-inch spring fuller. Check and recheck the height of each leg. Drill two 3/16-inch holes in each leg; check your layout to make certain the holes line up properly.

Forge four cross members from 3/8-inch square. Develop a 3/16-inch tenon 3/4-inch long on each end for riveting the cross members together.

Forge weld the top frame from 3/16 x 3/4-inch flats. Drill 1/4-inch holes in each corner of the frame.

If desired, gently hammer the corners of all of the parts; this "breaking the edges" gives a pleasant visual effect. It also provides subtle facets for polishing. Now that all of the parts have been forged, it is easier to pre-polish them unassembled.

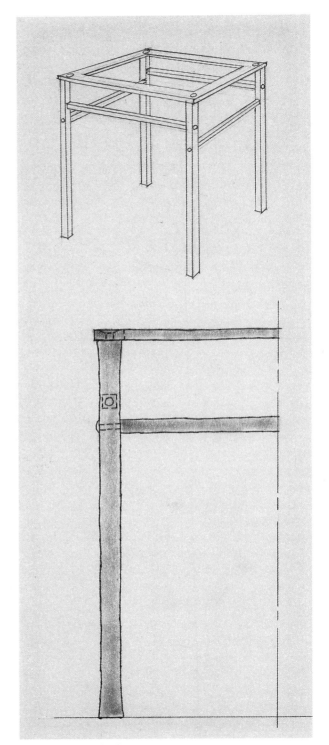

Table sketch and schematic.

80

To do the riveting for the table, it is best to use an oxy-acetylene torch. With this torch, you will be able to selectively heat just the end of the rivet to be headed as many times as needed. It is also a great help to have a level, metal-top layout table to set up these parts for final assembly.

Assemble two legs in pairs together by riveting the top cross members; then assemble these pairs together by riveting the lower cross members. Check and recheck alignment. Rivet the frame to the tops of the legs. Do the final polish and finish with the oil-wax finish. Select a glass, wood or stone top to suit.

Candle Cup

Make a cupped form, such as a candle pan, from sheet metal by forming it over a stake. This technique is good for forming a lip on a bowl. Make a stake from a rod that is 1-inch in diameter. Round off the top and shape the bottom, so that it fits into the hardie hole in the anvil or into a vise. If placed in a vise, the stake will be higher and at a better working height. Hold the sheet metal with tongs. Heat it, and place it on the stake. A dark spot will appear almost immediately on the top where the top of the stake cools the metal. Strike off to the side of the spot with the edge of your hammer, as you rotate the piece gradually. The metal will be gradually worked down. The edge of the hammer causes a slightly dented surface texture which will polish nicely.

Make a candle cup or holder by using the end of the stake to swage open the end of a 3/4-inch thin gauge tube. (Conduit is galvanized and when heated gives off toxic fumes; use only black tubing.) Heat the end of the tube and flare it over the end of the stake by hitting it with light blows. Do not work the iron below a dark red, because it might split. Take several heats to get the tube to flare out. After the lip is formed and the metal is cool, place the flared edge on the edge of the anvil and spread it further with a ball peen. Cut off the

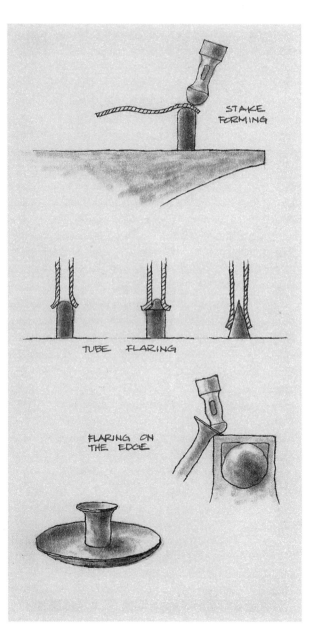

Steps in candle cup fabrication.

STAKE FORMING

TUBE FLARING

FLARING ON THE EDGE

cup with a hacksaw, when it is finished. Join the cup and pan together by brazing or soldering. (Brazing is the process of melting brass to join the pieces, whereas, soldering is joining with a tin lead alloy; see "Soldering" in the Resources section.)

Design a base and assemble to the cup. This type of assembly can be used for making candelabra with multiple candle cups.

Many of these processes are similar to the techniques used by silversmiths. However, the iron can be worked hot or cold, while the silver is worked cold. It is useful to study some books on making jewelry and silver smithing.

Sheet Metal

After sheet metal has been cut, it usually has a raw sharp edge. The standard method for eliminating this effect is hemming. It is simply folding over the metal on itself. This not only provides a cleaner safer edge but strengthens the part. A decorative approach is to cut a patterned edge prior to hemming the edge. This is useful for escutcheon plates. In this process a pattern must be developed, that is, a drawing which is laid out flat showing the complete pattern prior to bending.

Try several different sized pieces and of different gauges. Start with the lighter gauges of 22, 20 and 18. As the gauge numbers get larger the material thickness decreases. (See "Gauge Sizes" in the Resources section.) For this exercise, it is handy to cut out a paper pattern and glue it to the metal. Then the part can easily be cut out with chisels, saws or shears. After cutting out the part, the edges should be filed and the part put in the fire. Develop an even coating of scale and hammer finish as it cools. This creates a surface texture for polishing.

To bend the sheet metal, small pieces can be clamped in a vise and hammered over. For wider pieces, bending bars can be used. The bending bar

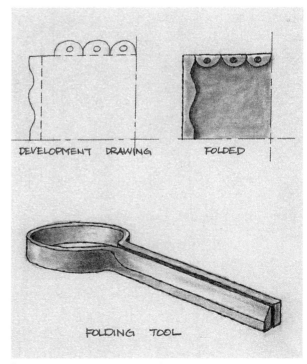

Sheet metal hemming and a folding tool.

can the be either clamped in a vise or held with "C" clamps. For sharper bends, the metal can be incised on the outside bend, and although this weakens it slightly, it creates a crisper look.

To make the sheet metal bending bar, use 1/4 x 1-inch stock or heavier. Form in a similar fashion to a spring fuller. One of the legs of the bar is normally 90° for making right angle bends and the other leg is ground to an acute angle. This allows the metal to be bent over for hemming.

Repoussé and Chasing

The first step in repoussé is to trace out the design on the metal using a tracer, a small sharp edged chisel. Cement a copy of the design on the metal and gently incise the lines. The incised lines should just be indications on the back side, but not too deep to break through. Heat the sheet metal and use the guide lines to form out a bulge on a swage block or a wooden stump.

Turn the piece and back up on a solid form, of wood or lead, in the bulge area, so that the form can be shaped from the front. This may have to be done several times to develop the preliminary shape. Once this is completed, the final chasing step can be done.

Backing up now must be done in a more secure manner with a shaped block of wood, sand bag or with pitch or lead cast into the back side. The material depends somewhat on the design, but generally lead works well. Melt the lead in a heavy pot and pour into the back of the form. Allow to cool. Chasing can be done on the front. Using modeling tools, punches and matting tools the final design can be executed.

Pitch for backing up can be made by this recipe:

Burgundy pitch	8 parts by weight
Linseed oil	1 part by weight
Pumice or plaster	add for density

Incising

Many soft metals like aluminum, copper and silver can be easily incised cold. Iron can be to some extent but it is much easier to work hot. Light incising on small pieces or on sheet metal can be an effective decoration and this is normally done cold.

When iron is hot, it provides a base for a wide variety of incising possibilities. On several bars of 1/4 x 1-inch iron, experiment with different incised patterns. Chisels and punches for this type of decoration can be of almost any form or shape. Try different angles on the cutting edges; this will give a different degree of spreading of the lines. After making several decorative bars, polish and wax them. Evaluate the effect of the chisels and the decorative patterns.

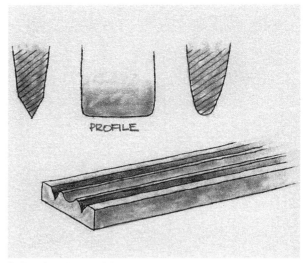

Fullered and incised lines.

A Leaf

The leaf pattern comes from an example of what can be done with the tools and processes described above. The material dimensions are no longer important, but what *is* important is how you see the part being forged. Make this part, polish and finish it. Then examine what are the qualities of the material and the process that you have used. Now is the time after this type of insightful examination to design and plan your own projects.

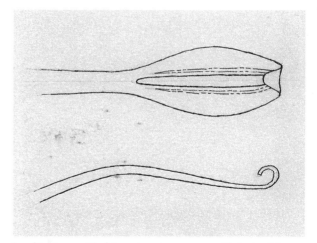

Leaf pattern with fullered center groove with incised lines on each side.

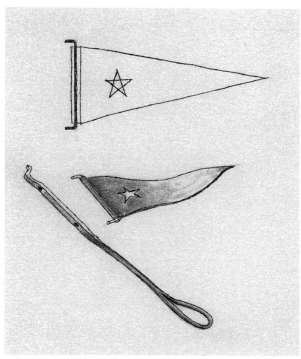

Pennant pattern and assembly details.

Star Pennant

To close these exercises, let's make a simple star pennant celebrating the work and toil, the fun and joy, and the future that blacksmithing holds for you.

Cut out a triangular pennant shape. Heat in fire and hammer on both sides. Do not clean off the scale from the anvil; this will give a texture to the sheet metal. Layout the five points of the star and make center point marks at the points. On a cutting block, cut out the star with a straight chisel. Ten chisel cuts will make the star from the center point layout.

Hem the edge of the pennant that is to be attached to the shaft, but do not hammer down. In the hem, place a 1/16-inch brass rod and close the hem over the rod. Bend the ties over and leave excess on the ends. On a wooden stump with a ball peen hammer gently form the waves in the flag.

Make a staff of a welded handle and flatten the top of the staff. Drill two clearance holes in the flat for the brass ties. Insert the brass ties, cut off and rivet these ends. Polish and oil.

Wave the pennant and celebrate.

Metallurgy for the Blacksmith

Metallurgy is the science and technology of metals. It concerns the extraction of metals from their ores, the refining of metals and the relationships between physical and mechanical properties of metals and their composition, mechanical working and heat treatment. Metallurgical information is helpful to any blacksmith, whether he is doing general blacksmithing or tool making. If you are a general blacksmith, then you need only understand the very basic principles; however, if you are a tool smith, then you will need a broader understanding. This does not mean that you will have to be a metallurgical engineer to make good tools, but that with some metallurgical knowledge, you will be able to select the correct material, forge it properly and heat treat it to develop the desired physical properties.

The basic forging processes are made possible because the iron becomes plastic and can be forged when it is heated to a cherry red and above, up to a light yellow. Iron can be welded when it is heated to a light yellow. When heated to a dazzling white, iron begins to melt and "burns;" this destroys the metal for forging purposes.

The structure of iron and all its alloys is crystalline. Plastic deformation of crystals is possible through the generation and motion of crystal defects called "dislocations." These deformation processes operate with less deformation force as the temperature of the iron is increased. Thus, when iron is heated, it becomes more plastic. Generally, the higher the heat, the easier it is to form the metal.

A piece of iron is actually composed of many individual iron crystals, called grains, each having a different orientation of its crystal axes in relation to the neighboring grains. Normally, the grain size is too small to observe without the aid of a microscope. Sometimes, a fractured piece of iron will show evidence of the individual grains of iron that are visible to the unaided eye. The grain size is very important for determining the strength of iron: the more refined (smaller) the grain size, the stronger the iron and the tougher (resistance to fracture on impact) it is.

There are two factors affecting the grain size that the smith can control at the forge: the temperature of the metal and the nature of the mechanical working (forging). The diagrams of grain size (a-c) illustrate what happens to the relative grain size of iron when it is heated to a dark cherry, an orange and a light yellow, then allowed to cool without any forging. It is easy to see that the higher the temperature, the larger the grain size.

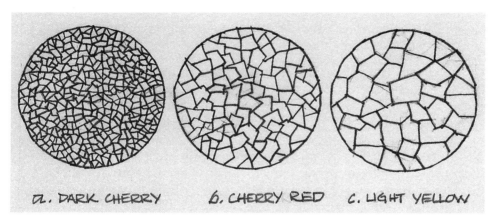

Chart 1. Grain size of iron heated to different temperatures.

When iron is heated and then forged, the forging refines, or makes the grain smaller, as in (a). This hammer refining must continue until the iron cools below the critical temperature. If the forging stops before the iron is cherry red, or the iron is reheated without further forging, the grain growth will resume, as in (b).

Welding heat greatly increases the grain size (c). However, the weld can be hammer-refined (a) to break up the coarse grain. With this type of control at the forge, the smith doing general metal work can resolve most problems.

Mild steel can be used for simple tools only. As a tool designer you must use special steels for tools that will be tough, hard and durable. To create these steels, alloying elements are added to the iron. The major alloying element added to iron is carbon. The chart of maximum attainable hardness shows the effect of increasing amounts of carbon in steel. Steels with only 35 to 45 points of carbon can be used where moderate hardness is required. (Steels begin to respond to heat treatment with around 35 points of carbon.)

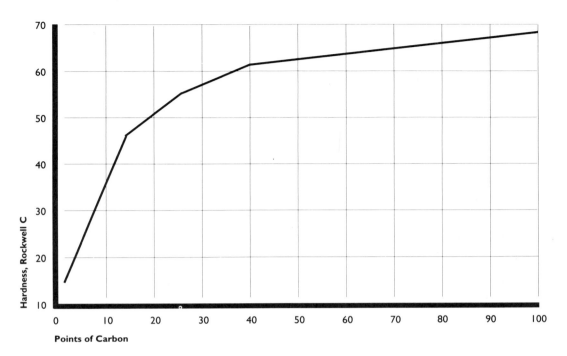

Chart 2. Maximum attainable hardness of a quenched steel relative to the carbon content..

Hardness is the ability of a metal to withstand being deformed by indentation. This can be measured by a machine called the "Rockwell hardness tester." There are other tests, however, only the Rockwell C hardness scale will be referred to here. A relative degree of hardness can also be determined by a file. (See "File Test" in Resources.)

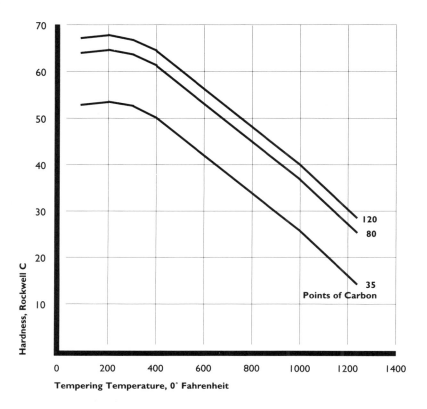

Chart 3. Effect of carbon content of three different steels.

Chart 3 shows another relationship of carbon to iron: the differences of tempering temperatures on the hardness of three different steels for equal tempering times. Notice that there is a greater difference of hardness between the steel with 35 points of carbon and the one with 80 points than there is between the steel with 80 points and the one with 120 points.

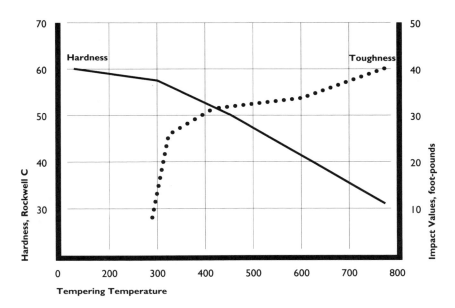

Chart 4. The relationship of toughness to hardness in O-1 tool steel.

Toughness is the ability of a metal to absorb energy and deform plastically before fracture. The Izod impact machine measures toughness. Chart 4 shows the relationship between toughness and hardness as a function of tempering temperature. It is easy to see that there is a trade-off of toughness for hardness. Note the very steep curve as toughness increases to 30 foot-pounds.

These are some of the observable properties of steel. What causes these to happen and what factors are used to make these changes?

The first test that you will later make is the center punch and is to determine the temperature at which to quench the metal to harden it. This temperature is called the "critical point" or "critical temperature." Why is this so important and what happens at this temperature?

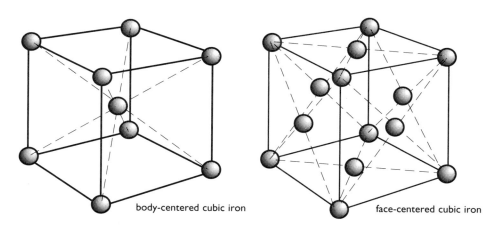

body-centered cubic iron   face-centered cubic iron

Diagrams of the different cubic structures or phases of iron.

On heating, the crystal structure of iron changes at the critical temperature from the body-centered cubic structure to the face-centered cubic structure. The face-centered cubic crystal has spaces between the iron atoms that can easily accommodate carbon atoms. Very little carbon can be accommodated in body-centered cubic iron. When an iron-carbon alloy is slowly cooled through the critical temperature, a carbon-rich "iron carbide" phase is precipitated; at the same time, new grains of the body-centered cubic iron are formed. However, if the alloy is cooled rapidly (quenched) the face-centered cubic structure transforms to the body-centered cubic structure so rapidly that the carbon is trapped inside the body-centered cubic crystals. These crystals of metal are now in a highly stressed condition because they have cooled and changed shape and are supersaturated with carbon atoms (sort of a pregnant crystal). This makes the metal very hard and brittle. The degree of stress can be controlled by reheating the metal (tempering) and the desired physical properties of the steel can be tailored to the task. Tempering also allows for the precipitation of sub-microscopic metal carbide particles that strengthen and toughen the steel. Putting the steel in the stressed state is hardening, removing some of these stresses is tempering, removing all of the stresses is annealing. These processes are referred to as "heat treating."

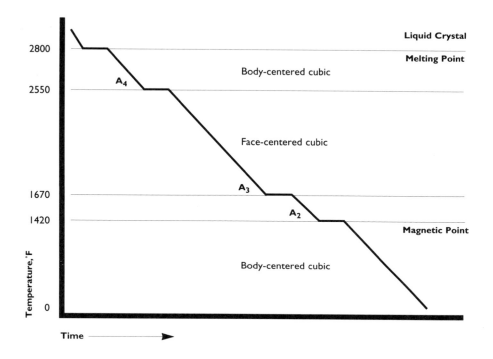

Chart 5. Tempature curve of iron on cooling.

Another way of looking at this is to plot a temperature curve of iron in Chart 5. When iron is heated or cooled, the crystalline changes show up on the curve as steps or temperature arrests; these points are labeled A_2, A_3 and A_4. Notice that at A_2 not only does the crystal form change, but the metal loses its magnetism. The smith can use a magnet to determine the critical temperature for high carbon steels. Place a magnet on the steel; it is at the critical temperature when the magnet no longer holds.

The major factor that influences the critical temperature of steel is the amount of carbon it contains. The phase diagram of carbon steels, Chart 6, shows these relationships between carbon content, the ranges over which the different crystal structures are stable, and the various critical temperatures. The horizontal scale shows the amount of carbon in the alloy and the

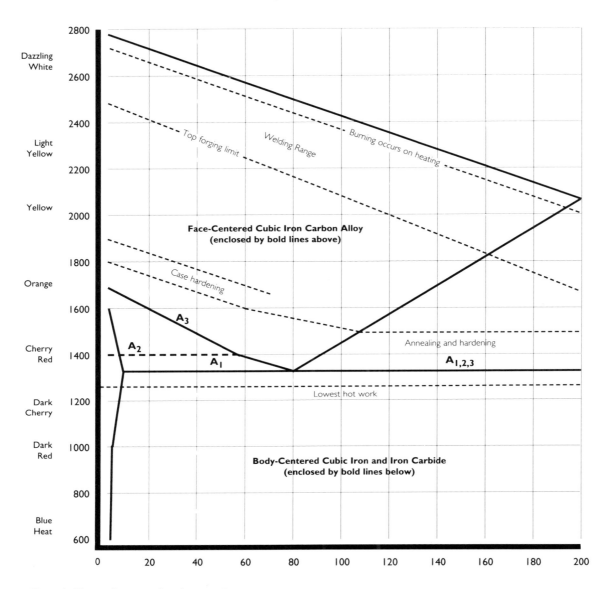

Chart 6. Phase diagram of carbon steels.

vertical scale shows the temperature. From Chart 5 we know that point A_2 is the critical temperature (where the phase change occurs); on the phase diagram it is a line, intersecting with A_3 and then A_1, as the carbon content increases. Thus we can use this chart to determine the critical temperature of known steels.

The following temperature ranges may also be determined: for forging, for forge welding, for case hardening and for annealing and hardening.

The Basics of Heat Treating

With this background of information, let us proceed to an explanation of the practical aspects of tool making. As we have seen, there are three different steps in heat-treating steel: annealing, hardening and tempering.

The simplest heat treatment is annealing, which is heating the metal to just above the critical temperature and holding it at that temperature to heat the metal uniformly, and then cooling it slowly in a dry medium, such as fine sand, ashes, lime or vermiculite. Annealing softens the material by relieving any internal stresses caused by forging or excessive heat. Annealing is sometimes necessary to sufficiently soften a piece for a cold shaping operation such as machining or heading a rivet. Generally, annealing temperatures are kept low so as to avoid excessive grain growth. Notice the area on the phase diagram, indicating the range of annealing and hardening. Some tools steel require that they be annealed to be properly hardened and tempered, some do not. (Check the recommendations by the manufacturer.) The general rule is to anneal all tools after forging.

Hardening is the process of heating the metal uniformly to a top temperature slightly above the critical point (A_3) and quenching (cooling) it rapidly in a suitable medium. When you are heating the steel to be hardened, you must have a reducing fire and must heat the piece uniformly; heat it slowly and turn the piece frequently to get a uniform heat. Do not take the metal too far above the critical point (no more than 50° F. above) for it will only increase the grain size and weaken it. When the critical point is reached throughout, quench the piece immediately. Quench on a rising heat, not a falling heat; in this way, you will not enlarge the grains excessively.

To harden steel, it is important to cool the metal quickly. Different media give different cooling rates. Those most frequently used are listed in the order, beginning with the fastest: 10-percent brine solution, cold water, warm water, cold oil, warm oil, and still air. Use the proper quenching medium for each steel. If you use a quench that cools the steel too rapidly, it will create excessive stresses and cracks will form. To avoid this, a slower quench medium should be used.

The mass of the piece is another important factor in the hardening process. A small, thin piece, like a knife, will cool quite rapidly, but a heavier, thicker piece, like a hardie, will cool much more slowly, regardless of the quench medium, because the heat has to be drawn through the metal; the cooled part acts as an insulator. The rate at which a piece cools is important. It must cool quickly enough to harden properly. To offset the problems caused by slow cooling, use a steel that contains alloying elements in addition to carbon. The desired physical properties will then be maintained. The ability of the iron to be hardened in depth consistently is hardenability. Hardenability is increased by the following alloying elements, listed in order of decreasing potency: boron, manganese, molybdenum, chromium, silicon and nickel.

It is important to understand the difference between the maximum hardness obtainable in a steel and its hardenability. In plain carbon steels, the hardness is a function of the carbon content only Chart 3, whereas hardenability is concerned with the depth of hardening.

Temper Color	°F	Tool
	660	
Steel grey	650	
	640	
Greenish blue	630	Light Springs
	620	
Light blue	610	Screw Drivers
	600	Wood Saws, Punches
Dark Blue	590	Springs
	580	Picks
Blue	570	Cold Chisels, Light Work
	560	Knives
Dark Purple	550	Cold Chisels, Steel
Purple	540	Axes, Center Punches
Light Purple	530	Hammers, Sledges
Brown with Purple Spots	520	Surgical Instruments
Dark Brown	510	Twist Drills
Bronze	500	Rock Drills, Hot Chisels
Dark Straw	490	Wood Chisels
Golden Straw	480	Drifts, Leather Dies
Straw	470	Pen Knives
Straw Yellow	460	Thread Cutting Tools
Yellow	450	Planer Tools
Light Yellow	440	Drills for Stone
	430	Paper Cutters, Lathe Tools
Pale Yelow	420	Razors
	410	Burnishers
	400	Scrapers

Chart 7. Temper colors for various tools.

After a piece has been hardened, it should be tempered as soon as possible. A hardened piece is very highly stressed and can easily develop cracks if it is just laid aside. For the same reason, do not drop it, for it might shatter.

The temperature at which the temper is drawn is determined by the function of the piece and the desired properties. The effect of tempering a fully hardened carbon steel is shown in Chart 3; it can easily be seen that as the tempering temperature increases the hardness goes down. The result of this is shown in Chart 4, which shows the trade-off of hardness for toughness. Understanding this relationship is very important for the blacksmith making tools. A cold chisel must be tough and yet remain sharp, a razor must be extremely hard in order to hold an edge and a spring must be flexible and durable.

Chart 7 of Temper Colors gives oxidizing colors for a temperature and the tool for that range. This chart is a guide, and it is advisable to test out your tempers for the tools you are making because of the many variables that can change the results.

There are several methods for raising the temperature of steel to be tempered: a furnace, hot oil, molten lead, gas torch and the forge. The furnace offers the greatest control, since it can be set up with temperature controls. Hot oil has limits, because it will catch on fire if it gets too hot, but its temperature can be controlled easily. The gas welding torch is particularly useful when you are tempering the sections of a piece differently, but it is very hot, so be careful. The forge is used for most tempering and with experience, just about anything can be done at the forge. The limitation is the smith's ability to recognize the oxidizing colors and judge the temper temperature from that.

To temper flat springs use a heated pan of fine sand to heat the piece and draw to the desired color. Linseed oil boils at 600°F., which is a good temperature for saws.

Another method for drawing a temper is called "flashing." This is used to temper springs in the blue colors (around 600°F.), for oil flashes (catches on fire) at this heat. Dip the piece to be tempered in the oil and put it on top of the coals in the forge; move the piece around to get an even heat. When the oil flashes, quench the piece in the oil. Repeat this process several times to develop an even temper on the entire piece.

When making a tool that must be tough and strong, use a steel that contains one of the following alloying elements (listed in order of decreasing potency): titanium, vanadium, molybdenum, tungsten, chromium and manganese. These alloys refine the grain of the steel and give it the necessary toughness and strength.

Forging and Tempering Colors

The charts of forging and tempering colors are usually separated, but they have been combined here in an attempt to clarify this aspect for the beginning smith. The two ranges of colors should be learned. Experience is the best teacher.

The incandescent forging colors are created when iron is heated in the forge. However, describing any color verbally is virtually impossible. Added to that is the variable that colors appear different when viewed under various lighting conditions. This creates a problem in identifying the color for the critical temperature 1420°F. (This is also the transformation point A_2, shown on Charts 5 and 6.) It is easy to determine this temperature at the forge. As iron is heated and reaches the critical temperature, it becomes non-magnetic. Hold a magnet on the iron and when it looses its magnetism, that is it. You can thus be assured of this point, regardless of the lighting conditions where you are working. This cherry red is the fixed unwavering point, for your conditions, against which all other temperatures and colors are relative.

The temper colors are created on the surface of a piece of polished iron when it is heated. The colors are a result of oxidation; as the temperature increases, the color becomes darker because of the increased rate of oxidization. A rainbow of colors is created; these are indicated on an expanded chart along with the temperature and the type of tool that is to be tempered. Viewing conditions also affect these colors, although not as much as the forging colors. However, there are several variables which do affect these colors: the manner in which the piece is polished or ground, the presence of any surface film of wax or oil, the shape and mass of the piece, the time it takes to heat it and the type of fire used to heat the piece. (Some fires or torches can cause a film on the metal, creating a false reading.) Heat several different thicknesses of metal; in this way you will be able to see the colors and the way in which they change.

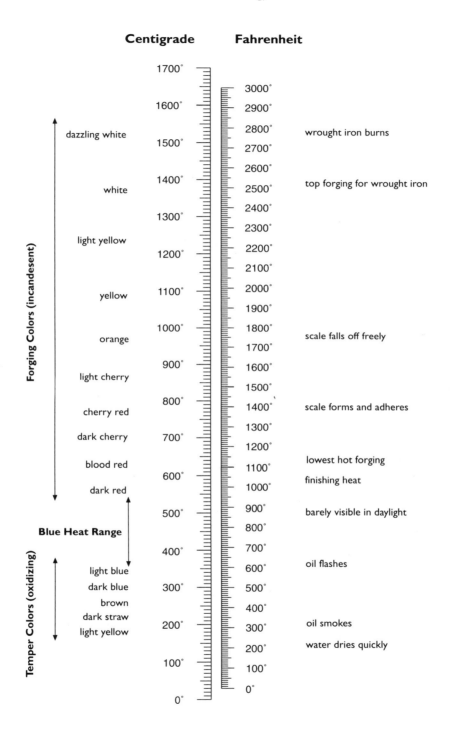

Chart 8. Temperature scales and ranges of incandescent and tempering colors.

Decarburization

Decarburization is the diffusion of the carbon in the steel to the surface, where it burns off in an oxidizing atmosphere. The surface of the metal loses carbon and some of its important alloying elements. This is no problem with low carbon steels, but is with medium carbon and tool steels, therefore, it is important to keep the forge fire a reducing fire, and to use as few heats as possible. Steels vary in their rates of decarburization. The decarburized skin can be removed by grinding operations. If you remove about .010 to .020-inch of the metal surface, this will clean off the decarburized metal. This is the normal amount required to dress most tools, knives or special parts.

Carburizing

Carburizing is the process by which carbon is absorbed into the surface of the metal by heating it above its critical temperature (A_2) while it is in contact with carbonaceous materials. This is also referred to as "case hardening," since the carbon penetrates only the outer layer of the metal. With proper heat treatment, a hard case is created, with a tough internal structure. This is useful on parts where wear-resistant surfaces and impact or shock resistance are both required. Carburizing can also be used to case harden the more forgeable mild steels after they are formed, or on steels where decarburization would be a problem. Mild steel with 10 to 25 points of carbon can be carburized successfully. Steels with a higher concentration of carbon become excessively brittle during this process. If this is not a factor, then use the higher carbon steels. There are special alloys for carburizing.

To carburize the finished metal, pack the pieces with the carbon materials in a steel box or pipe. (Do not use plated or galvanized pieces because toxic fumes will be created on heating.) Seal the container to prevent the carbon from burning off and use a box that is heavy enough to withstand the heat of a long fire in the forge or furnace. Pack the metal pieces evenly in the box with a uniform layer of carbon materials around them. This assures even heating and uniform carburizing. Usually a 1-inch space between the pieces is adequate.

The carburizing agents must be of a fine, even-granulated form, so that the carbon gases, CO and CO_2, can move freely throughout the container and into contact with the metal. It is the carbon gases, not direct contact with the carbon, that allow the carbon to migrate into the steel.

Commercial carburizing compounds are available, but you may want to mix up your own. In general, the mixture can be reused. The rule of thumb is to mix 1 part new to 3 parts used. The carburizing agents are: wood, charcoal, animal bone charcoal, charred leather, barium carbonate, sodium carbonate, calcium carbonate and sodium chloride. (The carbonates increase the activity of carburizing.) There are many other carbon materials that will work and can be tried, but you should not use any materials containing sulfur or phosphorus (use only charred bones). Charcoal will not be active in the carburizing process for long periods of time, so you should use bone-based materials in addition to the charcoal to sustain the carburizing process. Oil, tar or molasses are sometimes used as binders in the mixture.

A mixture to use is:

Hardwood charcoal	55 %	Charred bone	75 %
Barium carbonate	20 %	Hardwood charcoal	15 %
Sodium carbonate	15 %	Barium carbonate	5 %
Calcium carbonate	10 %	Oil binder	5 %

Place the container in the fire and bring it up to the critical temperature, turning the container so that it heats uniformly. You can place test wires through small holes in the container; these can be removed and checked for incandescent color temperature to determine when the interior comes up to the proper heat.

The depth of the carbon penetration is determined by two factors: time and temperature. As an example, on a piece of mild steel that is held at 1600°F. for seven hours, the penetration will be 1/32-inch. As the temperature is raised in 50° steps, it takes one hour less for the same amount of penetration. Thus at 1800°F., it takes only three hours for 1/32-inch of carbon penetration. (This would be about 85 points of carbon.) However, the higher temperatures will increase the grain size of the metal, so you must decide what factors to control.

If the piece being treated does not have to be shock resistant, then you can take it directly from the container and harden it by quenching it in water or oil. If maximum refinement is desired, then use these steps for a 1020 steel:

1. Carburize at 1650°F. for time desired and allow to cool in the box.
2. Remove and reheat to 1550°F.; quench in water (refines core).
3. Reheat to 1400°F.; quench in oil (refines case).
4. It can now be tempered at around 300°F.

Heat Treating Tools

With this beginning background of metallurgy and heat treating, let's make several tools which will be heat treated to attain the appropriate physical properties. You will come to realize that in blacksmithing, you can make many of your own tools, and that it really does pay to do them properly.

Among mechanics, the blacksmith holds a unique position, he being practically the only one who makes his own tools. This he often does without any apparent aim at economy, beauty, or usefulness, if judged by the chunks of steel on the ends of handles to be found in the odd corners of a great many blacksmith shops. It would not be fair to put the whole blame on the blacksmith, as he is usually allowed but very little time either to keep his tools in repair or to make new ones; the result is that if ever blacksmiths' tools have had a high standard of efficiency they soon depreciate. Too much reliance seems to be put on the old saying: "A good workman can do a good job with any kind of tools." But when it comes to saving time, which is one of the most important points in modern manufacturing, the good workman with good tools comes out ahead.   [James Cran, *Machine Blacksmithing*, p. 5]

To start, find a discarded car coil spring from a garage or scrap yard. This steel has 60 points of carbon, is hard, tough and suitable for the simple tools. It will be sufficient to begin with. Later, get good tool steels and follow the advice given above by Cran.

When we make these tools, it is important to heat the steel evenly in a reducing fire. Rebuild your fire, if necessary. Heat the spring to a light cherry and straighten out a section about 24 inches long. Cut it off on the hardie and allow this piece to air-cool. (When you put aside a piece of hot metal, be certain that it is out of the way, so that you will not bump it or pick it up inadvertently and be burned.) Straighten out the remainder of the spring, cut it into 24-inch pieces, set them aside and allow them to cool. Do not quench them in water. When the first section that you have cut off is comfortably cool to pick up, bring it to a light cherry, cut the blast and leave it in the fire to soak in the heat for a moment. It is important to heat heavier sections of metal evenly, so that no fractures occur while you are forging. If the metal is heated too rapidly, it will be hot on the surface and cooler on the inside; this condition will cause it to crack internally while you are working on it. If, however, the piece has cooled on the surface and is hot inside, surface cracks can form. Therefore, you must be careful to heat the metal evenly.

Refer to the temperature Chart 8 (p. 99). The upper part of the chart indicates the incandescent colors or forging colors. These colors are used in the hardening step of heat treating. The lower part of the chart deals with the oxidizing colors or temper colors.

After the piece has soaked in the fire for a moment, turn on the blast and bring it to a yellow heat. Draw out the end of the bar, forming a taper 2-inches long and about 1/4-inch square. This is a test piece. While still hot, with an old file, make notches 1/4-inch apart. These are reference marks, enabling you to see the colors of the hot steel when it is quenched (cooled in water to harden). Heat the taper as indicated and look at the positions of the various colors on the taper, using the reference marks as a guide. Count the number of marks back to cherry red and dark cherry, since this will be the temperature range at which the piece will be quenched. It may be necessary to return the taper to the fire, if all of the heat has been lost while you

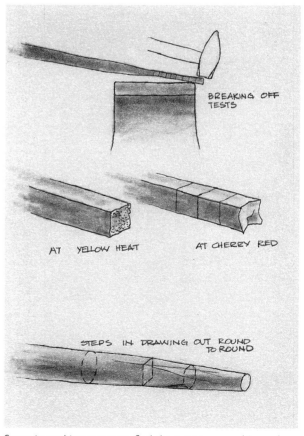

Steps in making a test to find the proper quenching color.

were studying the colors. When the piece reaches these colors and you can visualize them clearly, quench the piece by plunging the taper into water and swirl it around until it is cool. The piece has now been hardened.

Now we will look for the section that is in an optimum crystalline state. Place the first notch over the edge of the anvil and tap a shearing blow to the end. The piece will fly off easily. Examine the broken end and notice the granular quality. This is the crystalline structure of the steel. Move to the next notch and break it off. Notice the differences in the crystalline texture. It will be finer. (Keep the pieces and line them up.) Remember the colors at these points. Continue the process until you reach the piece with the finest crystalline structure, which will appear as a fine dull gray color. It also will break unevenly. Recall what the color was at that point, as this is the "critical temperature" for this steel.

Center Punch

You can now make a center punch with this piece. Since it is already drawn out, form a good taper which has a point that is 1/4-inch in diameter, cut off a 5-inch section and chamfer the top end. To bring the piece back to round after the taper is formed, develop the square section into an octagonal section and then forge it into a round section. If these steps are not followed, or a proper heat is not used, internal fracturing can result.

The forging process is finished and the steel should be annealed. Annealing is heating the metal to the critical temperature and cooling slowly by burying it in a dry medium, such as ashes, lime, sand or vermiculite. (Allow the metal to heat evenly and do not overheat the piece, or this will enlarge the crystalline structure and weaken the piece.) After cooling, it is annealed when it is cool enough to pick up. This will take some time, so go on to make some other tools of the same material. After annealing, heat treating is usually carried out in two different operations: hardening and tempering. It is sometimes possible to harden and draw a temper in one operation. Lay the tool on the fire with the punch end near the edge. You do this so that the thin part will not overheat. Heat it evenly and slowly, bringing it to the critical temperature previously determined by the hardening test. With a pair of tongs, grasp the center of the punch. Plunge the end into water about 2 inches deep, gently swirl it around for about 5 seconds. Move the punch up and down about an inch to prevent a water crack, a stress crack.

The metal is hardened. Quickly polish the end to bare metal, using an emery cloth, sharpening stone or bench grinder. The oxidizing colors will begin to appear on the surface of the bare metal closest to the end that is still hot.

Since you have studied the chart of temper colors, proceed immediately to the second stage of heat treating, drawing a temper. The cooler part of the punch is now being heated by the hot part and a thin layer of oxide is forming on the surface of the polished metal. These oxides are caused by the heat which oxidizes the part at a higher rate due to the increased temperature. As the hardened part heats up, this oxide film changes color from faint yellow to blue. This color change is an accurate indication of the temperature of the steel. When the punch becomes a light purple, you should quench it again. The end is now tempered. The heat has been drawn to the cooler end, thus, drawing a temper.

Change the position of the tongs and quench the head, the other end, for a few seconds to a depth of 1 inch; this slightly hardens the head. Stand the punch end down in a can of water 2 inches deep and allow the punch to cool completely. Test for proper hardness using the file test.

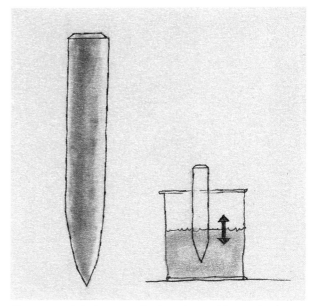

Center punch being quenched on the working end only.

A Safe Solution for Quenching Mild Steel

Sodium hydroxide has been used by smiths as the fastest quench medium for hardening steels. It surpasses cold brine solutions in speed of quench, however, it is caustic and very dangerous to use and is no longer recommended. Robb Gunter created a soap solution, which is safe to replace the sodium hydroxide. It is to be used with low carbon steels (no higher than 30 points). On a 1018 mild steel a tool quenched, at 1550°F. light cherry red, in this solution can reach a hardness of 43 to 45 Rockwell C.

5 gallons of water
5 pounds of salt
32 oz. Dawn Dishwashing Liquid (blue)
8 oz. Shaklee Basic "I" wetting agent

Finding new materials and processes to replace many of the old recipes and concoctions is important. Some of the original ones that I had previously used, which contained cyanide compounds and heavy metals, are replaced with other materials. They are dangerous to the smith as well as the environment.

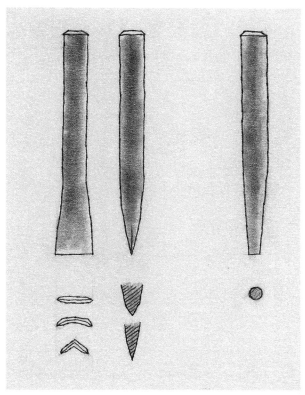

Chisels, hot and cold with different angles and a punch.

Punches, Chisels and Repoussé Tools

You can make other punches and chisels with the remainder of the spring steel. Refer to the diagrams and charts for sizes and tempering colors. The colors will draw faster when you are tempering these tools, because there is additional heat in the longer shank. You must work fast. Each of these tools should be dressed according to its use and need. When you are using the bench grinder, cool the tool in water frequently to prevent taking the temper out of the tool.

You may want to make a number of blanks for other punches for tools that can be used for repoussé. It is critical that these blanks be annealed prior to storing them. They will probably have considerable stresses from the forging and high heats, therefore anneal them to soften and to reduce the stresses.

Repoussé and chasing tools are generally smaller than the chisels; normally they are from rod 3/8 to 5/8 inch in diameter and 4 to 5 inches long. The faces are of many shapes and contours. The best steel to use for these would be a shock resisting steel in the S series. The tempering color for the S series steels is different than the steels just used, so some testing will be necessary. Other than that, they are made in the same way as the punches and chisels. (Refer to the drawings on page 40.)

While you are dressing the tools, bank the fire so that it will be ready when you return. Rake the coke in a mound over the fire and cover it with some green coal. (Or bury a block of wood in the center of the fire and bank it.) This will assure a new supply of coke when you return.

Eye Punch

An eye punch is a tool that is used to start the eye of a hammer. The eye drift is then used to give the final shape to the eye. The eye punch may or may not have a handle. The handle is usually set at a 45° angle to the line of the eye because this makes it easier to see the alignment when punching a hole. Use an eye punch that is about 50 percent smaller than the final size of the eye, so that you do not remove too much metal during the punching. Then the drift is used to open the hole. It is absolutely critical that the punched hole be centered and perpendicular to the stock. If an eye punch is not available, and you are making a small hammer, use a drill press to drill the hole and then a drift to shape the eye.

You can make a simple eye punch and drift from S-1 tool steel. Use the same method that you used in making other punches. Tongs or vise grips can be used to hold the drift; or make a longer drift which then allows you to hold the drift in place and work on the hammer.

Place a bolster under the piece when you are punching if the hardie hole is not a large enough hole in the anvil. Bolsters can be any size or shape.

Drifts

Drifts are forming tools that are used to shape a hole to the desired shape and size after it has been punched or drilled. The drift is hammered through the hole to shape the hole. Drifts are usually so plain and simple looking that they are mistaken for scraps or unfinished pieces. Hot work tool steel works well for drifts, since they get hot while in the hole they are shaping.

To make a square hole in a bar (as for the T-square) punch the hole with a punch. Hammer the square drift through the hole and dress up around the hole. Leave the drift in the hole when you are working around it.

For larger holes, a slitter is first used to open the bar. The slitter has a chisel end and sides; this starts the hole without wasting any material. A drift can then be used to open the hole to the desired size and shape.

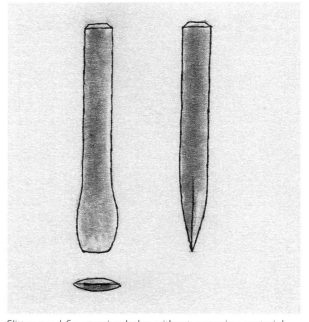

Tools to form a hammer eye.

EYE DRIFT   EYE PUNCH

Slitter used for opening holes without removing material.

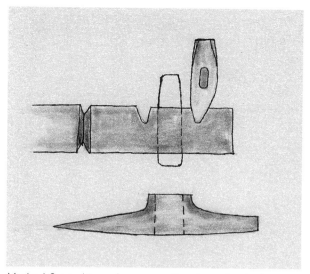

Method for making a hammer with a long shanked eye.

When cutting steel with a set hammer, it is important to align the hammer and the edge of the anvil with a slight offset, which shears the iron cleanly, rather than pinching it.

Rock Pick

A rock pick, claw hammer or a striking tool is made with a long-sided eye using the following technique: Use 1-inch by 3/4-inch tool steel. Punch a hole for the eye and open the eye with a drift pin until it measures 1 inch by 5/8 inch. Use a bevel set hammer to form notches on each side of the eye. This forms a shank on the head. Draw out the ends to form the head and pick. Work with a drift pin in the eye when you shape the side of the eye, the head and the pick. Grind the face and the point of the pick. Harden the head and draw to a dark blue temper.

Set Hammer

Set hammers are used to "set" or form angles and work the iron in tight spots where the face of the hammer could not make a clean hit. To do this, a set is struck with another hammer or sledge.

One might think that anybody knows how to make a set hammer, if every smith knows it, I don't know, but I do know that there are thousands of smiths who have never had a set hammer nor know its use. To make one: Take a piece of tool steel 1 1/4 x 1 1/4 inches. Punch a hole about two inches from the end, the hole to be 1 1/4 x 1/8. Now cut off enough for head. Make the face perfectly square and level, with sharp corners, harden and cool off when the temper turns from brown to blue. This is a very important little tool and for cutting steel, it is a good deal better than the chisel. Plow steel of every kind is easier cut with this hammer than any other way. In cutting with the set hammer hold the steel so that your inner side of the set hammer will be over the outside edge of the anvil. Let the helper strike on the outside corner of the set hammer and it will cut easy. The steel to be cut should be just a little hot, not enough to be noticed. If the steel is red hot, the set hammer cannot cut it. The heat must be what is called blue heat. I would not be without the set hammer for money, and still I often meet smiths who have never seen this use made of the set hammer. Plow points, corn shovels, and seeder shovels are quicker cut with this tool than any other way, with the exception of shears.
[J. G. Holmstrom, *Modern Blacksmithing*]

Small Hammer

We will now make a small, straight peen hammer. With a center punch, mark off a piece of tool steel (80 points of carbon) for the head. Bring it to a yellow heat and punch the eye. After several blows, remove the punch and dip it in water to cool it; at the same time check the alignment of the hole. When the hole is about 1 1/4-inch deep, dip the punch in a little coal dust before you return it to the hole. The coal dust will cause the formation of gases that will keep the punch from sticking in the hole as it is being hit. When you have punched the hole about three-quarters of the way through the head of the hammer, turn the head over and punch the hole through from the other side. Now, drive the eye drift into the eye. Leave the drift in as you work out the bulges on the sides of the head of the hammer. Draw out the peen. Make a cut three-quarters of the way through the bar at the face. Refine the shape of the head and cut it off completely. Bring the head of the hammer to the critical temperature and anneal it. When it is cool, dress the face and the peen with a bench grinder. The grinding removes the decarburized steel.

To heat-treat the hammer, take it to the critical temperature slowly, because the hammer is thick. Harden the face by dipping it in water to a depth of 1-inch; then turn the hammer and do the same with the peen. Quickly polish the face and the peen with emery and draw the temper on the face and peen to a light purple. Allow the eye to cool slowly. Dip the peen and the face alternately in water to maintain the temper. Set the handle.

The Striker

As you begin to work with larger material or as the projects become more difficult, you will need an assistant. The striker, or hammer man, is the smith's helper. He or she wields a sledge and stands opposite the smith at the anvil and strikes the iron under the direction of the smith. The striker should be a knowledgeable smith and understand the way in which the hammer is being

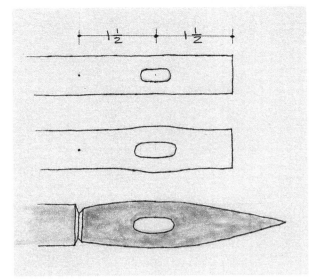

Layout for making a small hammer.

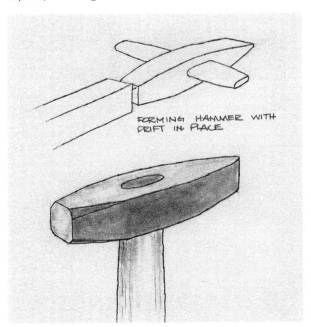

Small hammer.

used and how much force is being used. After each blow struck by the smith, the striker must hit the iron with their sledge in exactly the same spot, and at the same angle, but with a proportionately heavier blow. When striking, words are unnecessary; the language of the smith's hammer is the only direction needed. However, the smith must indicate when wishing to start and stop. Then, when ready to start, the smith will strike the anvil three times. When ready to stop, the smith will hit the anvil on the side of the anvil or will lay down the hammer, but only after the striker has hit his last blow.

While working, the striker must strive to emulate the force and direction of the smith's blows. Although using a heavy sledge, the objective is not to hit as hard as possible. The striker follows, the smith leads.

Sometimes, the smith will hold a tool, such as a punch, fuller or flattie, along with the work. The striker will then strike the tool. Here also, the striker must know how to hit with the proper force and cadence, and know when to start and stop. The striker also helps to maintain the fire, cut stock, get tools and organize things for the smith.

Sledges

There are two types of sledges that the striker can use. The first type is the up hand sledge, which has a short handle (28 to 30 inches) and weighs from 5 to 10 pounds. It is held in your right hand close to the head and raised to the height of your head when you strike. The end of the handle is held with your left hand. Do not slide or move your hands when you are striking. (This is called the up-hand position.) Although this position might seem awkward at first, you will soon find that it works well. Your right hand and both feet should be in the position that you use when you are working with a hammer.

The second type of sledge is the swing sledge,

Samuel Yellin working with a striker at the anvil in the Arch Street workshop in Philadelphia. The striker is working in the up hand position; notice how he is gripping the sledge.

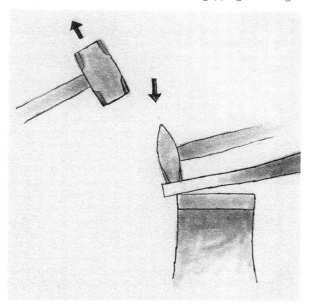

Movement of smith forging and the striker using a sledge.

which has a long handle (34 to 36 inches) and weighs from 8 to 20 pounds. Hold it and swing it like an ax, in a full arc. There will be considerable force created and you will not have as much control. Sometimes more than one striker will be working, especially if the piece is very large. Then you will need a heavier, larger anvil.

As the striker, stand opposite the smith at a distance that will allow you to strike a good blow and then draw back slightly, as you raise the sledge and prepare for the next blow. Both the smith and the striker must work in rhythm as they alternate blows, being careful to keep hammer and head out of the way of the next blow. Your stance must be balanced; stand approximately as you normally would, but with a wider secure stance.

Practice striking with a friend using a piece of hardwood. This way, you learn by doing and you will soon develop a rhythm. Drawing out is an excellent beginning exercise. Start striking and try to work in an even, steady cadence. Speed up slightly and then slow down. Try striking blows of different force and direction. Next, try tumbling while you are drawing out, keeping in mind that the smith must turn the piece before his blow only, never before the striker's blow. Otherwise, the striker would not know where to hit.

Anvil Tools

Anvil tools are much easier to make when you have a striker to help. The extra force of the sledge offsets the difficulty of working with heavier sections of tool steel.

To make a hot hardie, select a high carbon steel square section that is at least a 1/2-inch larger than the hardie hole. If you do this, you can easily form a shoulder on the tool to prevent it from jamming in the hole. (Use W-2 tool steel with 85 to 95 points of carbon which has good hardenability.) Fuller on the sides and draw out the shank to fit

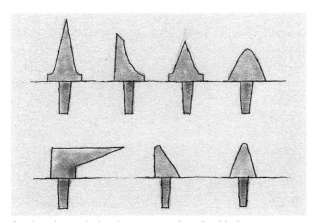

Anvil tools made by the process described below.

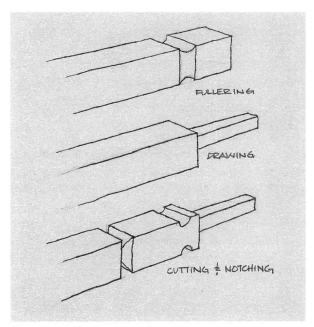

First steps in forging an anvil tool.

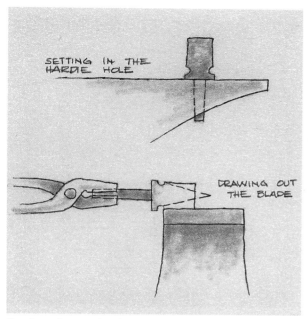

Shaping a hot cut hardie.

the hardie hole. Place the shank in the hardie hole, and then strike the top with a sledge thereby upsetting the shoulder and seating it. Make certain that the piece is perpendicular to the anvil when you begin. Also, rotate the piece 90° after four or five blows, so that it seats in all positions.

With your spring fuller, fuller a notch 3/8-inch from the shoulder. Cut off the piece 1 1/2-inches from the shoulder. To finish the piece, hold it securely by the shank with a pair of close-lipped or square-jawed tongs. Draw out the blade. Dress the cutting edge on a bench grinder.

It is best if these tools are annealed, then hardened and tempered. The cold hardie can be drawn to a purple, and the others to a blue.

Make the other anvil tools in the same way, but do not fuller a notch for the shoulder. Fuller only one side of the cutoff hardie.

Wrenches

Closed or open-end wrenches are handy. You will undoubtedly find a situation where a special size or handle shape is needed.

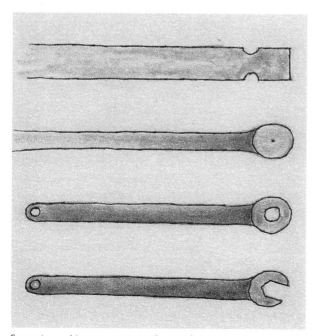

Steps in making an open end wrench.

To make a 1/2-inch open-end wrench use a 1 1/4-inch by 3/8-inch mild steel bar. Form notches with your spring fuller in the wide section. Draw out the handle and cut it off at 6 inches. Form the handle and punch a hole in the end. Now turn to the head. Trim the corners of the head with a hot chisel and shape it to a circle. Punch a 1/4-inch hole that is slightly off center. Using a hexagonal drift, and working from both sides, open the hole till it is a 1/2 inch in diameter. If it is to be closed, don't cut. Cut a slot for the jaws at a 20° angle. Form the jaws on a saddle. Use a flatter to dress up the sides of the jaws. Carburize the wrench as described on page 100. Carburization hardens the surface of the jaws, making them wear well and preserves the tough core.

Knife Making

There is a little forging involved in knife making, but there is a lot of bench work. It is rewarding, because during this process, steel is brought to a highly refined form. The procedure can be broken down into the following steps: design, selecting the proper materials, forging, shaping and finishing the blade, heat treating, assembling the blade and handle, shaping the handle, final buffing and sharpening.

Decide what type of knife you need and make several sketches. Trace the shape of the blade onto a piece of cardboard and cut out a blade template (or pattern). The template will serve as a guide at the forge for both the shape and the size of the knife. It is difficult to judge without it, because the blade always looks smaller at the forge (and in fact, may actually be much too large).

Select an alloy steel that is tough, that will hold an edge, and can be forged. Knife makers have found several tool steels that are excellent; these are W-1, O-1 and D-2 (see "Tool Steels Chart"). Chromium and vanadium are two alloys which, in addition to carbon, will provide knives with edge-holding ability. When you buy tool steel, remember to get manufacturer's instructions for heat treating and to follow them.

If corrosion resistance is important, the 400 series of stainless steels can be used. They are heat treatable, but 440 B and 440 C are the only ones that have sufficient carbon for knife making. Stainless has a very limited forging range, so you must be very careful when you are forging it.

Old files and car springs may be used successfully. However, they lack the additional alloys previously mentioned, and do not hold an edge as well. If you use a file, the teeth must be ground off first. Sometimes, because there is excessive sulfur in the steel, old files will crack when they are heated and forged. The steel is then called "hot or red short"

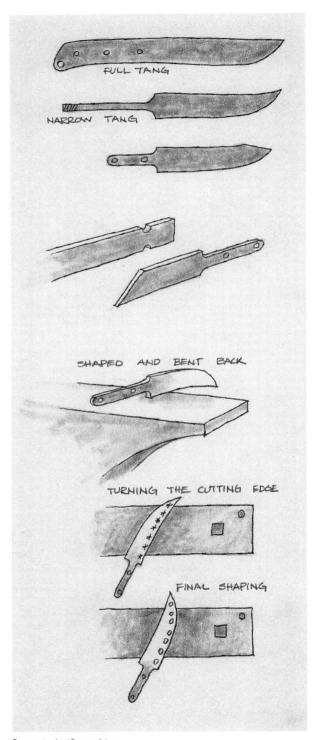

Steps in knife making.

and is not forgeable. Using worn files, old straight razors and leaf or coil springs is a way to get started. Eliminate the problems associated with these materials and become familiar with the wide range of tools steels available today.

Make a half-tang knife, using W-1 or O-1, by shaping the tang first. This is the narrow extension, which will later be enclosed by the handle. (Make it the length of a 3/16-inch drill, because you will later drill a 3/8-inch hole in the wooden handle.) Notch the metal with fullers and draw out the end, forming the tang. Be careful not to damage the radii formed by notching; they will prevent stress cracking later during the heat treating. Then punch or drill the rivet holes in the tang. (The wooden handle will be attached to the tang by rivets later.) Now turn your attention to the blade of the knife. Bend the knife blade blank into a curve. The cutting edge is the edge on the inside curve. Strike this inside curved edge with a hammer, working from the tang on out. As the curved edge is flattened, it will gradually straighten out. At the same time, draw out and taper the blade. Use a flattie or a finishing hammer to refine the surface of the blade, making certain that you do not work the metal below the recommended forging heat. Keep the scale brushed off. Make certain that the blade is straight, as this is the last of the forging operations. Anneal the blade.

Remember that during the forging operations the surface of the blade will decarburize (i.e., lose carbon). This can be ground off during the shaping operations, but remember when forging the blade to use as few heats as possible and a reducing fire.

Place the template on the blade, and trace the outline on the blade with a piece of chalk. Grind the outline to shape. Check the taper and thickness.

The degree of finish that you use on the surface of the blade may vary from a highly polished one to one that has the forging marks left in. Finish the

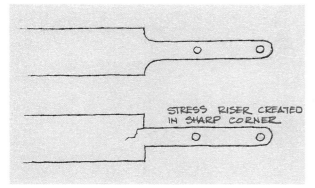

Stress crack in a corner that is too sharp which creates a stress riser.

blade with a belt grinder, which is better than a grinding wheel for this type of finishing. Shape and finish the blade completely, but do not do the final buffing. This will be done after the heat treating.

After finishing the blade, heat treat it in a fire of well packed coke. You can also use charcoal in the fire. Keep the blast low.

Lay the blade on the fire and bring it up slowly to hardening heat. Turn it frequently. Be certain that it comes up uniformly and do not overheat it. Watch the point; it is thin and easily overheats. When the blade is at the proper color, quench it by placing it edge down in the proper medium.

After the blade is hardened—temper it immediately. A pot of oil makes a uniform tempering medium, but you will need a high temperature thermometer to take the temperature. You can also use an propane torch to temper a knife. The torch offers flexibility, because you can move it over the blade and control the heat. (The flame is hot, so work slowly and carefully.) Temper the parts of the blade differently. The tang and top of the blade should be the toughest parts, the middle of the blade should be harder and the edge of the blade should be the hardest.

To temper the blade in the forge fire, make a sheet-metal cone and place it in the fire. Temper the blade by moving it back and forth. (I prefer the fire to the torch since there is more control and less heat.) Temper colors for knives range from yellow to light purple, depending upon the knife's use. Draw the temper on the tang to a light blue.

Another method of drawing a temper is to use a heavy block of metal that has been heated in the forge. Lay the knife on its back edge on the block and draw the temper. This is perhaps the safest method, but you must still be careful of overheating the point. If the knife is overheated then repeat

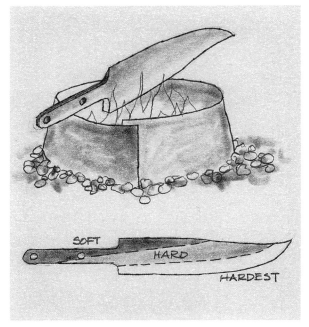

Tempering a knife over the forge fire.

the process and return to the hardening step. Small parts can also be tempered in this manner.

There are limitless possibilities for your knife handle. If you prefer a knife guard, make it of brass or nickel silver. Both of these metals can be soft-soldered to the blade, if the soldering temperature is kept below the temper temperature. To make the handle, drill the holes for the rivets. Attach it to the blade with epoxy and rivets. Finish carving and sanding the handle.

When the handle is finished, you can buff the blade. Be careful not to overheat the blade (and thus take out the temper) as you are buffing it. Sharpen the blade on successive grades of oilstone, ending up with a hard, fine stone. The beveled edge of the blade should form an angle of 10° to 15°, depending on the knife's use, and your own personal preference.

Advanced Knife Making

Knife makers today has advanced to a level of technology, craft and artistry which is incredible. Not only are they rediscovering ancient metallurgical processes but creating new ones. The material that they work with is generally called Damascus. This name is derived from the swords and knives brought back from the Middle East. Also called pattern welded and wootz Damascus blades this is an advanced metalworking area and beyond the discussion of this book, but perhaps not beyond your aspirations in the metal arts.

Corrosion and Protecting Metals

Metals are rarely found in their pure metallic state but are in combination with other nonmetallic elements. Metal ores are generally found in an oxidized form of the metal. The natural state of iron is iron oxide, Fe_2O_3. In the process of making iron, oxygen and impurities are removed, and basic cast iron is produced. Since this is not the natural state of the iron, it has a strong tendency to revert to its natural form, iron oxide or rust, by the process of corrosion.

Corrosion

Corrosion is the interaction of the metal with its environment that affects the physical properties and deteriorates the metal. Galvanic corrosion is the basic electrochemical reaction of the metal and its environment. This reaction is a flow of electrons in a galvanic cell where an electrical current is generated. Physical and chemical reactions occur within this cell of which there are two types: the bimetallic couple and the concentration cell.

The concentration cell occurs in the same metal or alloy and consists of an anode, cathode and a return current path. Differences in the concentrations of the solutions contacting the metals provides the electromotive force.

The bimetallic couple is similar to a battery composed of two dissimilar metals in an electrolyte. When the two electrodes are connected by the electrolyte, an electrical flow is created.

In these galvanic cells, there are four aspects which are necessary for corrosion to occur. First, an anode is created where the reactions generates electrons. This is where corrosion occurs. Second, a cathode is created which receives the electrons. No corrosion occurs at the cathode. Third, an electrolyte must be present which conducts the ion current. Electrolytes include water solutions of salts, bases and acids. Fourth, a return current path must be present between the anode and the cathode which is a metallic path, usually the underlying metal.

These four factors are the basis of corrosion. Removing or modifying any of these factors will prevent corrosion. Substituting a different metal for the anode may cause the current to reverse resulting in a change as to which electrode corrodes. Selection of the proper metal for the anode becomes important. The list below lists metals by their decreasing electrical activity. Metals on the top have a great tendency to lose more electrons than those metals on the bottom. Zinc, from a practical standpoint, is an ideal choice for the anode.

Corroded End, Anode

Magnesium
Zinc
Aluminum
Cadmium
Steel
Alloy Steel
Cast Iron
Lead
Tin
Nickel
Brass
Bronzes
Copper
Nickel-copper alloys
Stainless Steel (passive)
Silver
Gold
Platinum

Protected End, Cathode

Chart 9. Electrical activity in metals.

Corrosion is controlled by many factors. Some are pH of the electrolyte, electrical potential and resistance between the anodic and cathodic areas, temperature and humidity. Others factors in steel which effect corrosion are uneven internal stress, impurities, variations in composition and a variable environment.

There are two basic ways to protect iron from corrosion: cathodic protection and barrier protection. In cathodic protection an element in the corrosion circuit is changed or added insuring that the base metal to be protected is the cathode. An example of this is placing a zinc mass on the bronze shaft of boat propeller to protect the underwater metal parts. Another example is coating steel with zinc or galvanizing (discussed later). This method is called the sacrificial anode method.

Barrier protection is the oldest and most widely used method. It acts by isolating the iron from the environment. Paint, wax and oil are the most widely used products.

Wax and Oil Finishes

The simplest method that you can use to protect a piece of iron is to brush it briskly with a wire brush, to remove the loose scale, and then to rub it with linseed oil or wax. When the iron is warm, the oil and wax can penetrate under the edges of the scale, forming a protective barrier. This is an interior type of finish and may wear off with use, but it is easily replaced. Later you may want to repeat this process. It is even better to use a combination of linseed oil and beeswax for most objects. To a pint of boiled linseed oil that has been thinned with 1/2 pint of paint thinner heat slowly while adding a 3 to 4-cubic-inch lump of beeswax. Stir until the wax melts. Use by heating the part, so that it can still be held, and apply this mixture. Allow to cool and then rub with a soft cloth. Later paste wax can be used to help keep the iron from rusting. Two good paste waxes that can be use are Johnsons and Butchers wax. Both provide a soft luster to the metal.

To create a finish that has an aged quality, coat the part with boiled linseed oil. After you apply the oil to the iron, hold the piece over the fire, so that the linseed oil will carburize slightly; or if the part is small put it in the oven and bake it for 10 minutes at 300 F°. After the part is cool apply another coating of wax and rub. However, bear in mind that when you are treating objects that will be used in or around food, vegetable oils should be used. When using linseed oil, it is best to use boiled rather than the raw oil. Boiling it starts the polymerization of the oil, and it will harden much faster.

Removing Scale

"Hammer finishing" is gently hammering the iron as it is cooling, the heavier deposits of scale are worked off and a fine surface is developed. However, if you want to make certain that all the scale is removed, you can use mechanical or chemical methods. Use a wire wheel, an abrasive wheel or a flap wheel; these wheels also polish the iron as you remove the scale. These wheels work well for pieces that are simply shaped and that have flat surfaces that are easily accessible to the surface of the wheel. However, you may not be able to remove all of the scale on more intricate pieces, particularly in the crevices and corners. For those pieces, you must resort sanding by hand, describes earlier in "Polishing."

If all of the scale is to be removed, it can be done by chemical means by soaking the piece in an acid "bath"; this is called "pickling." Be careful not to leave the metal in the bath too long; if you do, it will pit. You must neutralize the iron with a solution of baking soda and hot water or other buffering solutions. Wash it thoroughly in hot water after these baths. Be extremely careful when you are mixing, handling and working with the pickle solutions.

Below are several pickle formulas. Hydrochloric acid works faster than sulfuric, but it costs more. Phosphoric and oxalic acids do not leave a corrosive salt on the metal. Oxalic acid attacks only the oxides and not the base metal. All of these solutions work faster when heated.

1.	Hydrochloric acid	1 gallon
	Water	1 gallon
2.	Sulfuric acid	1/2 pint
	Water	1 gallon
3.	Phosphoric acid	1 pint
	Water	1 gallon
4.	Oxalic acid	1 pint or granular equivalent
	Water	1 gallon

Proper precautions must be taken when working with acids. Always add the acid to the water and wear protective clothing and a face mask. When heating these solutions—use the proper respirator.

The other methods for removing scale are by "sand blasting" and "shot blasting." This method cleans the scale completely from the metal. Sand blasting (usually silicone carbide sand) changes the character of the surface finish making it a dull grey. Shot blasting (small beads of steel) is more gentle on the surface and does not change the surface finish. If painting or galvanizing, then sand blasting is the best method, since it provides an excellent holding surface. If a natural finish is used then shot blasting (shot peening) is desired, since it gives the metal a natural metallic look.

Painting

If the iron work is to be used outside, you should consider painting to protect it. Make sure that the surface is clean; there should be no rust, scale, water, oil or grease. Prime the surface. A good primer is a must. Apply a light coat, making sure that it completely covers the metal. Spraying is better than hand brushing, because the air blast forces the paint into areas that cannot be reached with a brush.

Several aspects of a primer are that it has good adhesion qualities to the base material, and that paint has good adhesion to the primer. It should also cover well and can be sprayed and brushed. Short drying times are important. If it contains zinc or zinc compounds it will offer anodic protection. A different color primer from the final paint color helps in seeing if there is good coverage for the finish paint, which is usually black. But, that was a design principle that Henry Ford used years ago and I think there are a lot of other possibilities.

There are many good finish paints, ranging from glossy to matte. Recently great advances in paint formulations have been made and there are a wide range of paints systems that can be used. Everything from water-based systems to two-part polymer systems.

There are many firms that make a brush-on preparation for metal, which cleans and prepares it for painting. It can be brushed on and then wiped clean. The preparation does not leave corrosive salts, as do the acid baths; instead, it leaves a phosphate coating that helps paint to adhere to the metal. There is one disadvantage to painting the metal: the paint covers the natural texture and color of the iron. If you are going to use the piece inside, you can avoid this by painting it with a clear polyurethane varnish. This will give the metal a glossy satin or matte finish, depending on the varnish used. For variation, you can wire brush or highlight the iron with paint before varnishing it. If you want to highlight it with paint, clean it and then rub the crevices and corners with a rag damp with black or other pigmented paints. Using another clean rag, rub off the paint on the highlights. Allow this to dry before sealing it with the clear polyurethane varnish.

If any rust appears, clean the piece down to the bare metal, then prime and paint it. A spot of rust under the paint will continue to corrode; it must be completely removed.

Historically, there are many examples of iron, painted many colors and decorated with gold gilt. There are also many examples of metal product and devices painted and treated in all manners. Create your own method!

Blueing

Blueing offers a small amount of protection from corrosion. Its value lies in the aesthetics. I have used the term blueing to cover the topic of chemically coloring the surface of iron. We usually associate blueing and other coloring methods with gun smithing. Much of the best information on blueing comes from gunsmiths. Some excellent sources which will give you the fine points about this process are: *Modern Gun Smithing,* by Clyde Baker, *Metal Finishing Guidebook Directory* and *Phosphatizing and Black Oxide Coating of Ferrous Metals,* by the Department of Defense.

The colors are created by the following processes: chemical solutions which cause surface oxidation chemical solutions which change the surface of the iron into a different substance; and the combination of heat and chemicals, which cause oxidation. (See manufactures listing in Resources.)

You can use these processes on iron that has first been machined, polished, sandblasted or finished down to the bare metal. Clean it thoroughly to remove all oils and dirt. Any impurities will produce faulty coloration. First remove excess oils with a solvent and a clean cloth. Immerse the piece for 5 to 15 minutes in boiling water, containing 1 to 2 tablespoons of lye per gallon of water. When it is clean, immediately immerse it in clear boiling water for several minutes. It will rust if you do not do this quickly. Then, transfer it to the hot blueing solution, leaving it there until it reaches the desired color. Use wires to suspend the pieces in the solution. Rinse it in boiling water, dry it and rub it with oil. The blueing solution can be made in different concentrations:

Sodium thiosulfate	3 ounces
Lead acetate	2 ounces
Water (boiling)	1 gallon

Another blueing solution is:

Ferric chloride	2 ounces
Mercuric nitrate	2 ounces
Hydrochloric acid	2 ounces
Alcohol	8 ounces
Water	8 ounces

Use this solution at room temperature. Clean the piece as previously described and place it in the solution for 20 minutes. Remove it and let it stand at room temperature overnight. Immerse it in the solution again for

20 minutes. Boil it in clean water for 1 hour. Dry it thoroughly, brush with a scratch brush and rub it with oil.

A third blueing solution is:

Water	1 gallon
Phosphoric acid	4 ounces
Soft iron filings	1/4 ounces

Clean the steel of oil and scale. Boil the piece for 1/2 hour in the solution; rinse with hot water and dry; immediately oil or wax.

Galvanizing

For work that will be exposed to a harsh environment, galvanizing is the best method for protecting the iron. Galvanizing is done by dipping the work in a molten bath of pure zinc. The zinc not only completely covers the iron, but forms alloy layers of zinc and iron. During galvanizing, zinc and iron react with one another and form a metallic bond which is impermeable. Edges and corners are as thick as the coating on the iron. The aesthetic quality of the zinc is objectionable to many, but the material can be painted which further adds to the protection.

One of the problems with galvanizing is that there is usually a good deal of clean up work after the dip in the molten bath. But with proper design and consideration of using parts to form an assembly this can be partially overcome. (See the Resources section to get technical information from the Galvanizers Association.)

A Raven and a Swan

Not long ago, reading the Fables of Aesop, I came across the tale, "A Raven and a Swan."

Once a raven thought it would be great to be as white as a swan; he fancied that the swan's beauty was derived solely from its whiteness. He set about washing himself, he changed his diet and environment, and journeyed from his home to lakes and streams. But there the water was not good for him, the change of diet and environment took its toll and he wasted away and died.

To me the moral of the tale is this: certain specific properties and characteristics should not be altered or changed. The raven failed when he tried to make himself white. Iron is not necessarily improved when its intrinsic beauty is covered.

Portfolios

There are two metalworkers that I have selected from the past era of blacksmithing: Martin Rose and Samuel Yellin. They have been selected because they represent the scale and scope of the metalworking business from the turn of this century until World War II. They both have left a legacy of well designed and forged metalwork. Each had their own unique manner of operating a business and promoting it. It is men like this, both whom came with the skill and techniques they learned in Europe, that form the basis of knowledge for our craft today. To these men and their families continuing this work today, we owe a great debt. These men represent the familiar edge of the anvil.

Along with the historical past, I have profiled the work of six practicing contemporary metalworkers. The selection of these artists/blacksmiths was done to show a small cross section of the different types of metalwork being done in the United States today. Different attitudes and styles are represented, as well as different types of work and approaches. The common link of working metal links these six different artists: Elizabeth Brim, Fred Crist, Tom Joyce, Nol Putnam, Brad Silberberg and Enrique Vega. These metalworkers represent the other edge of the anvil.

Let the three kings represent the past, the present and the future of the metalworking arts. The past and present are known—the future holds great promise.

Three kings forged at the Yellin Arch Street workshop.

Martin Rose
Rose Iron Works, Inc.

An early Gothic door photographed in the Rose shop prior to being installed, 1929.

Martin Rose was trained as an Austrian-Hungarian smith and served his apprenticeship from 1883 to 1887. Subsequent journeyman's travels, in typical guild tradition, were rigorous, intensive, broad and above all disciplined. Included were all the necessary components for future success: structure, forging, repoussé, assembly and erecting. Additional formal training in art history, ornament, design, drawing and business management enhanced his acumen as one of the leading masters of his period.

Frustrated by excessive taxation, Rose closed his Budapest shop in 1901 and reestablished himself in Cleveland, Ohio in 1904, as Rose Iron Works Inc.

America's prevalent styles were ideally suited to his training and broad background. Able to meet and exceed expectations of the most demanding clients and architects, he prospered. He prided himself in producing anything requested in his shop with 28 men including his sons. Products included interior and exterior hardware, lighting fixtures, fireplace accessories, tables, grilles, balconies, railings and gates. Functional requirements and workmanship were his uppermost priorities. He was confident that his creative designing would satisfy any and all aesthetic demands.

Martin's versatile, sometimes eclectic, designs were acclaimed. Greatly influenced by Italian work, he emphasized negative open space "breathing room" as much as positive shapes. Repetitious "hackneyed" C or S scrolls and similar forms were unacceptable as he gave free reign to inventive forms and combinations.

While employing classic methods, he constantly explored new techniques and materials. These evolved from his insatiable curiosity about new technologies. Machining, oxy-acetylene, arc and later heli-arc welding he frequently utilized. Aluminum, stainless steel and Monel Metal were enthusiastically explored and incorporated into his ever-broadening palette of expression. Aesthetic and execution standard were, however, never compromised using new emerging methods.

Unique among American smiths, his art-deco work is widely acknowledged as equal to France's best. This resulted from the synergism of Martin and Paul Fehér, a designer he brought to America. Fehér also taught the Roses sandblast carving of glass. They were the first to incorporate decorative glass elements into their metal work.

Weathering the depression with only a nucleus of men and his sons Stephen, Milton and Melvin was traumatic. Changed architectural and life styles were almost a death sentence. Metal commissions were all too few. Pragmatism, adaptability and personal sacrifice were instrumental to their survival. The carved glass work which sons Milton and Melvin developed into substantial mural projects helped greatly.

World War II shut down all but war work. Former clients provided entry into a new world: industry. Martin's heritage of integri-

Study for Art Deco torchiere, ca. 1929.

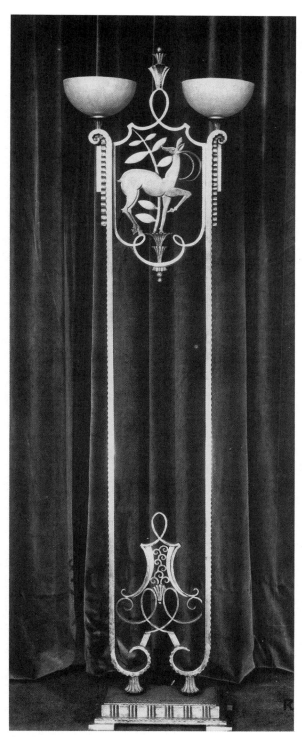

Art deco torchiere, iron and bronze.

ty, craftsmanship, profound knowledge of metals and above all adaptability provided his sons with the means for survival. A variety of forgings and fabrications of heat and corrosion resistant alloy, served the war effort.

Today Rose Metal Industries, Inc. doing industrial work, and Rose Iron Works doing major decorative work, are respected marks testifying to Rose versatility. A diverse group of individuals skillfully combine their ancient craft with computers and robots. The firm, 90 years young, blends art school and engineering graduates' creativity. Responding to renewed interest, selected decorative metal commissions join volume decorative metal housewares and industrial products. All thrive utilizing advanced manufacturing technologies.

Robert, Melvin's son having accepted "the key, hammers and anvils" and leadership responsibility, is building toward the 21st century.

Martin Rose's dream of a continuum of his beloved life's work is a reality expressed in their credo: "We want to be a significant part of those who keep our craft alive and worthy of the recognition it deserves and thereby make our mark."

All of the photographs and drawings are from the Rose family and Rose Metal Industries, Inc.

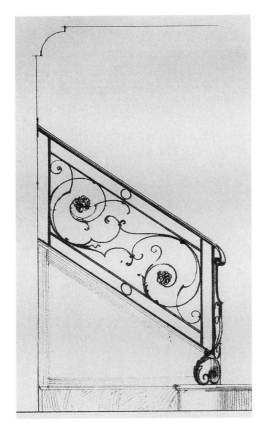

Study for interior iron railing.

Hardware iron, ca. 1917.

Interior iron railing, 1932.

Iron gate being set up to be photographed inside shop.

Study railing.

Art Deco iron and aluminum gate, ca. 1930.

Aluminum clock dial, ca. 1942.

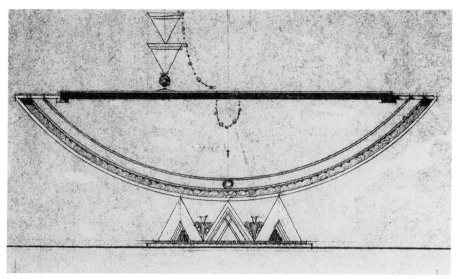

Study for table.

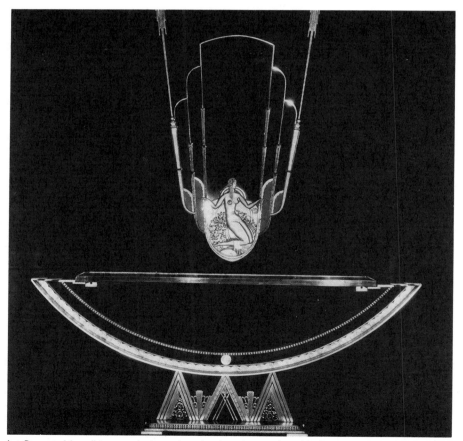

Art Deco table, all iron cadmium plated; mirror iron with gold plated bronze, ca. 1930.

Study for Art Deco entrance door, ca. 1934.

Art Deco screen with the iron silver plated and the bronze gold plated, 1934. (Photo by Randy Juster)

Iron mirror frame.

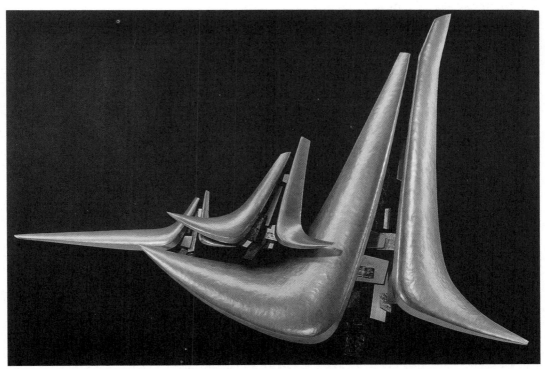

Repoussé gilded aluminum mural with patinated brass, bronze and copper, 1955. Designed by Paul Miller.

Study for well head, ca. 1933

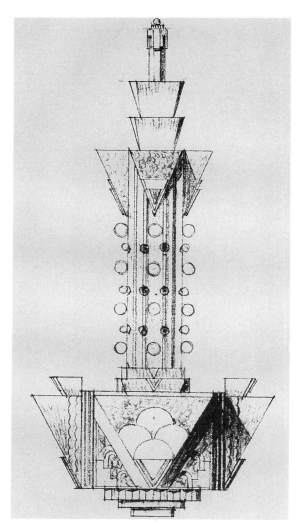

Study for metal and carved glass Art Deco chandelier, ca. 1933.

Interior iron gate, 1924. (8' wide and 5'6" high)

Samuel Yellin
Samuel Yellin, Metalworkers

Yellin loved the Gothic style and much of his work was devoted to that type of work.

Samuel Yellin was born in a small town in Glacia, Poland, in 1885. As a young boy, he was inclined to work with his hands and liked to draw. When he as 12 years old he was apprenticed to a Russian blacksmith in the town. Working with an unusual intensity he received his master's certificate in 5 years. At 17 he left home to travel throughout Europe to broaden his education and training as a blacksmith.

In 1906 he came to Philadelphia to live with his mother and two sisters that had proceeded him. He enrolled in the Pennsylvania School of Industrial Art (now the University of the Arts) to study, "The History of the Decorative Arts." His ability to work in iron was noticed by the instructor of the metals classes and he was asked to establish a class in "Wrought Iron." He taught the class for 14 years, later handing over his teaching responsibilities to his head superintendent at his workshop.

In 1909 he started his first shop; later moving to a larger space in 1911. In 1915 he moved to the workshop on 5520 Arch Street which was to be his creative studio until his death in 1940. In this environment he along with his designers and workmen he created an incredible amount of wrought iron commissions of extraordinary artistry, craft and quality. The peak of the shop came in 1928 when 268 were

Balcony on the corner of the Arch Street building.

employed at this atelier. This work today remains to remind us of the great power that wrought iron can bring to our buildings and environment. This may have been the height in the creation of architectural wrought iron.

Yellin died in 1940, and his family has continued to operate the business since that time.

The following photographs are a small selection of some of the examples of his work that was photographed in the Yellin Museum. They have been selected as examples to show the wide range of drawing and forging techniques used at the Yellin shop. These are examples that were made to show clients, and made as sample test pieces for the men in the shop. (For a complete account of Yellin's life and work see, *Samuel Yellin, Metalworker.*)

Yellin's personal entrance gate and door to his office.

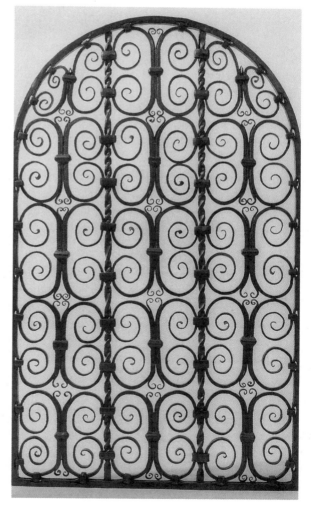

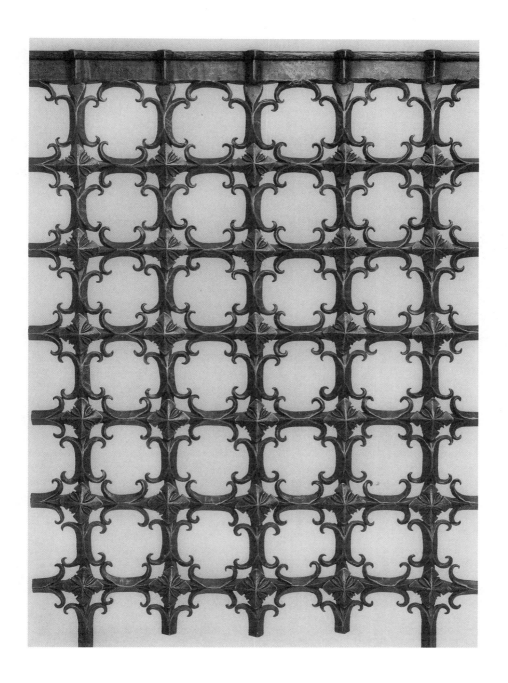

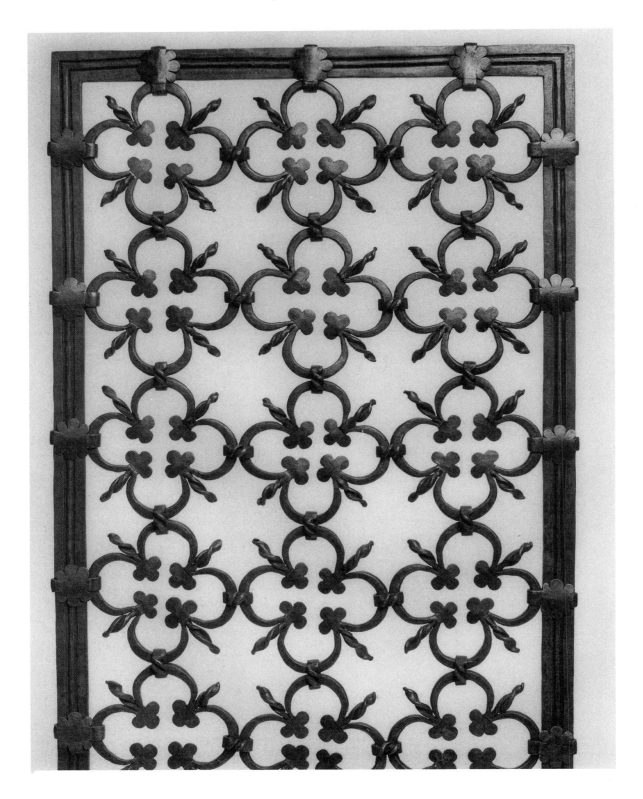

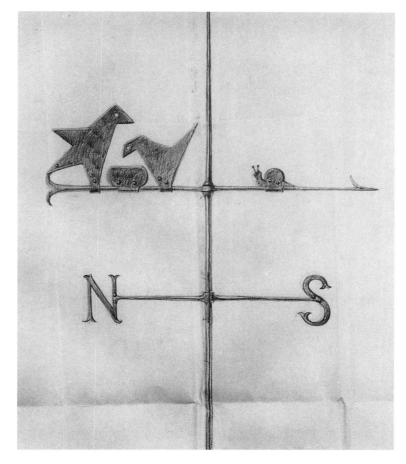

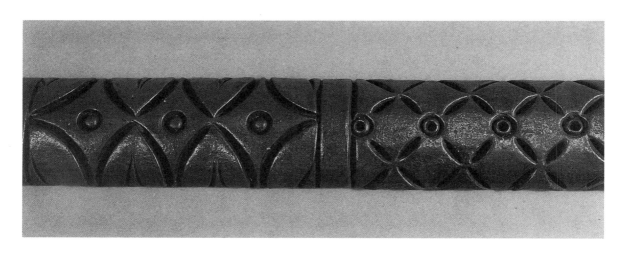

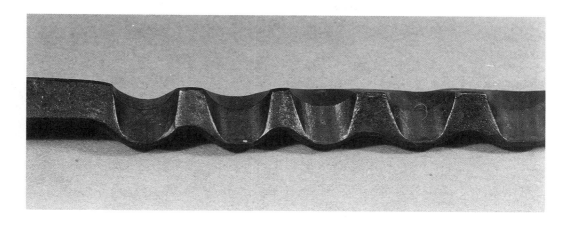

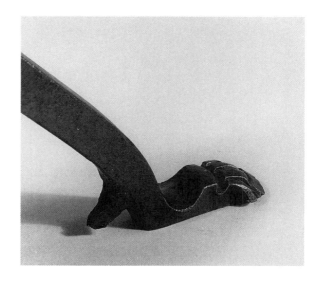

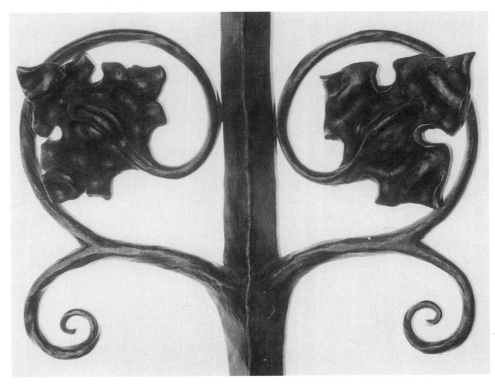

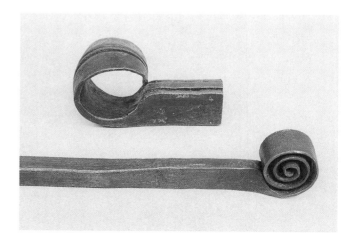

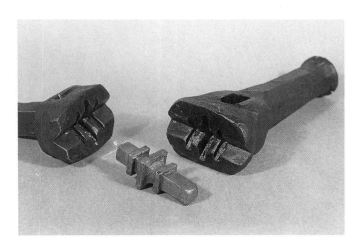

Elizabeth Brim
Sculptor

Forged iron apron.

Forged steel heels.

Elizabeth Brim creates her iron work in her studio in Columbus, Georgia. Although the scale and nature of her work is different than the other metalworkers represented here, her artistic intent is clear. At the 1994 Artist-Blacksmiths' Association of North America Conference, in St. Louis, she was asked to do a working demonstration. In a recent letter about the conference and her work, she wrote the following:

"I was very surprised to be asked to be a demonstrator at the ABANA International Conference. The tools and techniques I use to make things are, for the most part, basic and ordinary. I finally determined that the reason anyone would consider my work to be interesting or outstanding must be the imagery.

"I decided to take the opportunity as a demonstrator to encourage creativity and individualism in blacksmithing. I wanted to stress the idea of learning all the techniques one could and using those techniques to express a unique personal vision. Ideas, style and imagery are what makes individual pieces interesting and different—they make us curious.

"Ideas and imagery come from an individual's unique life experiences, attitudes and associations. Each one of us have a vast resource of information conscious and subconscious to draw from. Sometimes we are able to identify the impetus that stirs our imagination—triggers the creative impulse. Other times we are already in the midst of making a piece before we realize where the idea might have originated. It may be that we don't know or ever care where the resolve to make a certain thing came from or what caused the act of creating. Most of the things I make are for fun. The simple enjoyment of making something.

"The steel heels were a fun challenging project one of my first finished sculptures in steel. I made them as kind of a joke—a reaction to the fairy tale of the, 'Twelve Dancing Princesses.' I decided to make some indestructible dancing shoes so the princess would not be found out.

"Cultural associations enable use to relate or read images in artwork. The same personal vision and association that give individuality to a person's work colors their perception and understanding of other's images. It is very interesting to me to hear what someone find in my sculptures.

"I had always admired what I call tire shards while flying past them on the highways. One day I was driving and not in a hurry so I decided to collect some. I did not know what I wanted them for. Walking down I-185 with handsful of the material I looked at it and thought—this looks like a beautiful bouquet. At home I happily arranged them in a crystal vase and made steel lilies which were rusted to go with the rusted wire in the tire material.

"In the 1992 ABANA conference gallery we had a international panel do a walk through critique. Some members of the panel read a lot in and had a lot to say about the piece I had titled "Rust Blooms." They went on about the portentous dead look of the flowers—lilies symbols of funeral. They said it spoke of the future of the ecology of the earth. That it terrified them!

"The Japanese panelist were asked their opinion of 'Rust Blooms.' They said, 'Nothing in it, purely a decorative item.' That illustrates the differences in thought and symbology in our cultures.

"I had made a tiara and wanted a pillow with tassels for it to sit on. David Seacrest was teaching in the Penland Iron Studio and suggested I try forming a pillow with air.

"I cut two pieces of 1/8-inch thick sheet metal the same size, clamped them together and ground the edges so the pieces were the same shape. The edges of the sheets were... beveled with a grinder. The sheets were welded together leaving one opening big enough to get a chisel in. The opening is stretched so that a 3/4-inch pipe can be welded inside. The weld needed to be good but it is not necessary that the piece be absolutely airtight.

"This flat envelope was heated in a gas forge to bright red. An air gun was inserted in the pipe and I used about 90 pounds of air pressure to inflate the pillow. That was the first basic pillow form. It was fun to see it puff up. We all laughed a lot.

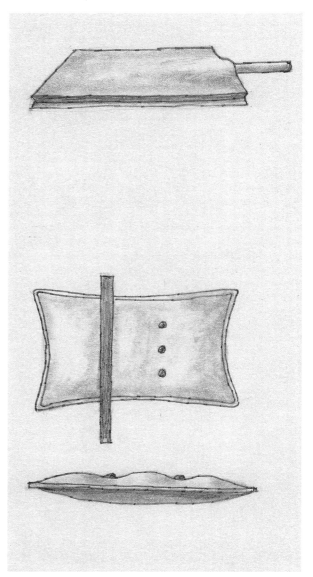

Steps in making a pressure formed pillow. Top view is the fabrication of the two sheets of metal and the installation of the air pipe. Bottom views are the hammering down the buttons (rivets).

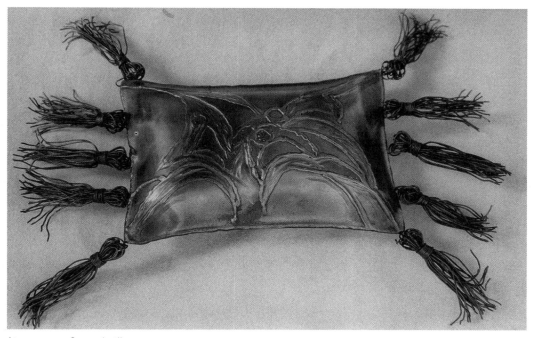

Air pressure formed pillow.

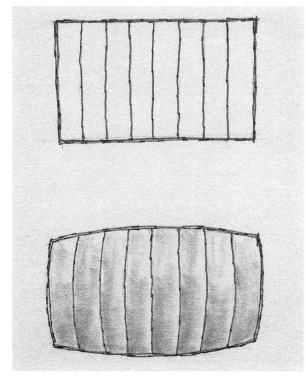

Pleated envelop pillow.

"Using this same technique steel 'buttons' are welded in the center of some. After the pillow is puffed up I heat around the button with a torch and knock the button back down. I use a wooden stick to form creases and knock the buttons back down. Spot heating and deforming the surface gives the pillow a softer look. I use rivets like buttons to create a pattern. Holes are drilled through the flat sheets. Rivets are inserted and welded from behind and ground flush....I heat around each rivet and knock it back down.

"I pleated some 20 gauge steel and then welded it together into an envelop and puffed it up. The pleating was a lot of trouble but it worked great when it was puffed—kind of like an armadillo.

"There are many variations still to be thought of in pressure forming. I want to encourage everyone to try it and anything that will serve to express ideas. The reason I use pressure forming is because I wanted to make a pillow. Don't let technique dictate your imagery or style.

"A lot of people at the conference told me they were going to use pressure forming. There were a lot of interesting ideas they were going to try. I am really looking forward to seeing the chickens someone had plans to make."

Fred Crist
Metalsmiths

Platen #II, forged steel plates and bars, 20 x 20 x 5-inches, April, 1994.

Fred Crist operates a forge studio in Waynesboro, Virginia with his partner Dave Munn where they are involved in designing and forging a wide variety of wrought iron commissions. All of the works revolve around the use of traditional techniques with the approach towards contemporary design applications. This interest in tradition carries over into the sculptural works which Fred is involved in, ranging from private to public work. Represented in a number of galleries and private collections though out the U.S.A. and abroad, his work is typified by the use of forged elements in creating spatial frames. And most recently a series which uses multiple plates and bars. These are forged, interlocking with one another creating 3-dimensional abstract planar images as the piece on the left demonstrates. Recently Fred discussed his approach to his sculptural work:

New forms are only the adaptation of tradition, viewed in a slightly different context of time and space. With this in mind, the Yellin studio inspired me to master the craft of blacksmithing, so that I could further explore the sculptural language of hot forging from my own direction.

For eleven years Fred was the head blacksmith at Samuel Yellin, Metalworkers. His main task there was doing all of the forging for the shop. This involved reconstructing many of the original Yellin techniques to be used for commissions that required duplicating the existing iron which had been done years earlier. There were also jobs requiring adaptations of Yellin designs to be used in situations that required him to make design changes. His research and study of the original Yellin techniques and tools lead to his rediscovery of many processes. These studies have led him to adapt to this body of blacksmithing knowledge to his own work.

The following forging demonstration comes from one of the original Yellin designs that was used in different applications. It represents one of the Yellin techniques that was used in which the metal bar was split out and then these splits were forged into a lighter more delicate forms. (See page 146 for a variation of this piece.)

In this design, consider the basic layout of each element on the bar and the overall visual effect of different spacing of the bars. First the bar is forged to proper size of 1 1/8 x 9/16-inch from stock 1 1/4 x 5/8-inch. (This step in forging the bar to size was called "reforging" at the Yellin shop.) The bar is then laid out and incised with a cold chisel in preparation for the splitting. This bar is based on a vertical module of a 3 3/8-inches.

At the top, split out each arm from the bar with a thin hot chisel. Cut off the top of the arm from the bar with a small curved chisel. Execute all splitting on the entire bar before continuing to the next operation. Keep straightening and truing the bar between each step in the splitting operation. This will prevent problems later.

Bend out the arm to extend 2-inches. With a set hammer, flare out the bottom part of the arm that is still attached to the main bar. Set the rest of this arm down from the main bar, so that the central bar is about 1/16-inch higher. Work both sides together and work on each module from the top down. One of Fred's comments learning to do this type of bar is, "If you do it the way I did in the original study, from the bottom up–you will have one hell of a time forging the offsets for the scrolls.

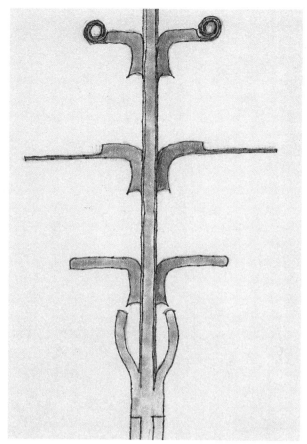

Drawing of the proper layout and working sequence.

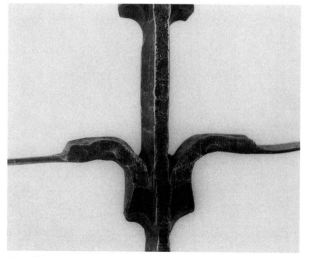

The offset arms drawn out ready to be rolled into scrolls.

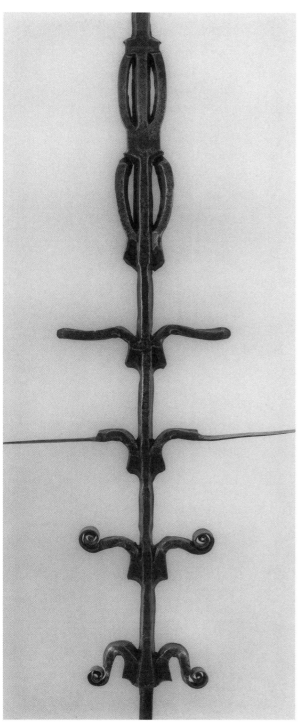

The steps in making the double scroll bar.

That is why we do studies!" (See the photo on the left.)

On each arm, form an offset of 1-inch and draw out a taper that is 3 1/2-inches long. Form this to a beveled knife edge as in the drawing below. Notice the the knife edge is open at the side facing the viewer and tight at the bottom.

Scroll each end. Bend a tighter radius in each arm to pull it in tighter to the bar.

When all of the arms are forged, true up the whole assembly. The bars may now be assembled in a frame. Plan ahead if tenons or rivets are to be used on each end of the bar to attach to a frame. Polish and oil.

An important aspect about doing studies such as this, is the sense of rediscovery. It can be a part of the creative process. Let it enable and free up your creative vision to develop new techniques and forms from the newly realized process.

Tom Joyce
Architectural Blacksmithing

A decorative screen for a home in Santa Fe. The genesis of the design was an autumnal seed head from a high desert grass in the area.

Tom Joyce built both his adobe smithy and home, in Arroyo Hondo outside of Santa Fe, New Mexico. It is a beautiful site and is designed to be compatible in its environment with rain water collection for an orchard and extensive edible garden, and a greenhouse to provide year round vegetables

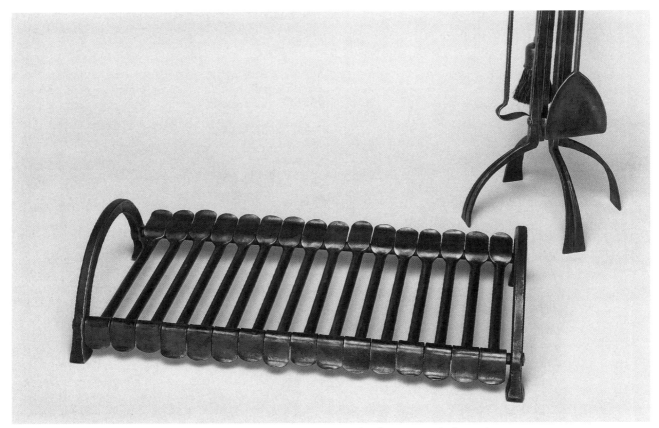

Arc fire grate with fire tools.

and solar heat for the home. All aspects of this place reflect Tom's attention to detail and his philosophy of life.

His early work as a blacksmith consisted of utilitarian objects, agricultural tools and repair and architectural forge work. The business grew to include a talented crew of five craftsmen. His commissions can be found throughout the United States, and he specializes in thematic design for building projects including hardware, lighting, furniture, railings, gates and all aspects of metal objects with seemingly no end to his creativity.

In a recent interview Tom spoke about his work:

While contemporary in design much of my work carries with it some form of historical reference which may not

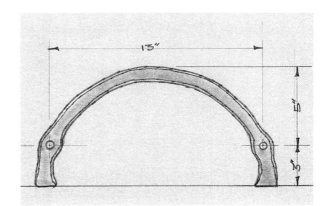

Layout of the arc and cross members.

182

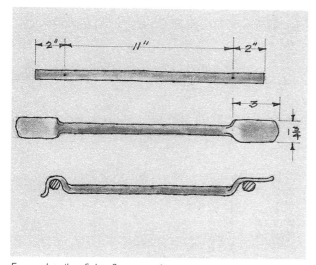

Forge details of the fire grate bars.

be apparent at first glance, but offers additional depth with which to read meaning into a piece. These designs also result form a need to satisfy functional requirements in seamless way, so that esthetic concerns are quietly addressed within the same functional detail and not merely embellished on to usefulness of the piece. Because these aspects evolve as one and often investigate paths towards unknown or unfamiliar resolve, new discoveries are revealed while integrating an historical precedence with a well founded yet hopefully fresh idea.

Tom Joyce continues to investigate the world around him and provide great joy to us in his art.

His fire grate is composed of two arced ends with two supporting cross members. On these supporting cross members rest the rotatable fire grate bars. This simple modular approach has led Tom to create a number of different types of design for this system.

The arced ends are made from a 3/4 x 1 x 26-inch bar on which all of the edges are chamfered. Each foot of the arc is upset 3/4-inch and bent in; a 1/2-inch diameter hole is split and drifted for the cross members. The bar is bent to the arc. The critical dimension is 13 inches from the centers of the holes for the cross members. (This dimension will vary with the depth of the hearth.)

The length of the 1-inch cross members supports can be sized relative to the number of fire grate bars. Allow 1 3/4-inch for each bar and add 1/4-inch slack on each end of the cross members. Tenon each end of the cross member and rivet to the arcs.

The fire grate bars are made from 3/4 x 15-inch round bars. Flatten and forge out 2 inches of each end of the bars to 3 x 1 3/4-inch. Bend these ends back to 90° and develop a shoulder. Bend back one end to a flat and bend the the other in the vise jig. With this fixture or jig it is much easier to make multiple pieces, saving time and producing uniform parts.

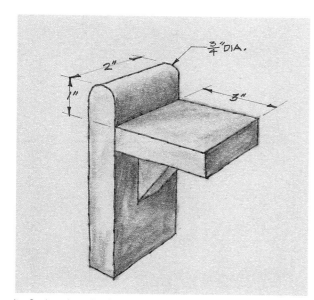

Jig for bending the loop on the fire grate bar.

Nol Putnam
White Oak Forge, Ltd.

West Columbarium Gate, Washington National Cathedral, Washington, DC, Installed 1993. (Photo Henry Eastwood)

Nol Putnam owns and operates the White Oak Forge in The Plains, Virginia. He specializes in architectural commissions: balconies, balustrades, stairways, driveway and garden gates. Nol often uses elements from nature to link the work with its surroundings, and has given a number of workshops on the forging of these elements.

The largest commission has come from the Washington National Cathedral for a series of three gates for the *columbarium*. The series started in 1988 and the final gate will be installed in 1994. The picture shown here is the major gate in this series. And the third is shown on the detailed steps on the next pages.

Largely self-taught, Nol's early years saw a lot of utilitarian work sold through a mix of local, regional and then national craft fairs. A small part of the work from the Forge is "house jewelry"—candlesticks, chandeliers, tables, fireplace accoutrements and the like. It is often a great relief to go from a six month project which has involved day work and night dreams to an elegant candlestick to be completed in several days.

Over the years, Nol has trained several people in his shop who have since gone on to their own endeavors. He now works alone. Moving into his seventh decade, Nol is forging, teaching, writing and drawing, trying to bring order to his work and interests—to make a whole out of the disparate parts.

Recently talking about the recent project for the Washington Cathedral Nol explained how he went about the project.

The sample of the gate prepared (third in a series for the burial vaults of the cathe- dral) for presentation to the client for approval.

On any large project, I always make a sample—to show the client, to work out the problems ahead of time, to know how much to bid the job. After the job is accepted, a full size drawing is the next step. With the sample and the drawing it is much easier to visualize the forging details and assembly problems.

Detail of cross member and collars.

The forging sample above is the part made for the cathedral which was the start for this project. The frame layout is transferred full size to a suitable table for assembly. Frame members 3/4 x 1 1/4-inch are forged and incised. Holes are predrilled, for the cross members, and the frame assembled. Vertical and horizontal cross members are forged from 5/8-inch square, incised and offset shoulders prepared. As these major pieces are fitted and sized for assembly, preliminary polishing is done prior to assembly.

Rivets, floral details, hinges and latching mechanisms are fabricated and all of these pieces are checked for the proper sequence of assembly. The basic frame members are then assembled by riveting together.

Collars and C-scrolls are forged and detailed. (Two weeks were required to forge out the scrolls.) They are laid out on the frame as completed. When all of the parts are finished then the final assembly is made. Each group of C-scrolls is fitted and collared in place. When assembled the final polishing and oil and wax finish applied.

The most recent driveway gate.

Brad Silberberg
Bradley Metal Design

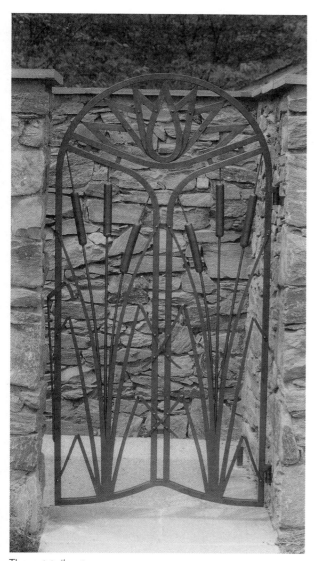

The cat tail gate.

Brad Silberberg operates Bradley Metal Design, Inc. in Silver Spring, Maryland on the outskirts of Washington, DC. He is a self-taught blacksmith, having learned his craft primarily from books and trial-and-error practice. A graduate of the University of Maryland Department of Studio Art, he has produced mostly architectural forged ironwork and furniture for the last 13 years. Now, he is trying to divide his time between architectural commissions and sculpture.

"I was making sculpture in wood, metal and stone long before I had never even heard of blacksmithing. I love the act of making these objects but felt that somehow something was missing—a purpose for their being. I began blacksmithing as a way to make tools for my artwork and fell in love with it. As I began to build architectural commissions I became aware that I was making art that was defined by its practical function, possessing a built-in purpose. Lately, I have come full circle, and am again exploring purely sculptural and less-than-functional forms in forged iron. Having mastered the manipulation of the material, self expression in and of itself now seems a valid purpose."

Brad has become an authority on the flypress, a type of hand-operated screw press more common in blacksmith shops in Europe and Great Britain. He uses flypresses extensively in his architectural work for bending, straightening and repeat forming. The fly press is used by many shops for small runs and jobs requiring specialized tooling. Although the flypress is hand operated it has the capacity to generate considerable force. He continues to explore their artistic use by employing

Vessel with top.

his 40 ton flypress to produce his "squashed containers." The flypress in this situation has the advantage over the power hammer because it exerts its force with a smooth action not an abrupt hammering action.

The vessel above started out as a 2 x 2 x 6-inch bar of mild steel. Heated in a gas forge furnace it was forged vertically in a power hammer to reduce the height by about 2 inches. This hammering was also done to create a surface texture. After repeated heats the piece was laid on the side and worked with tools to carve lines and indents on each of the sides. This was the preparation for the piece to be worked in the flypress.

At the fly press the iron was centered under the pointed ram and driven in. Brad and his assistant used repeated thrusts of the ram to start opening

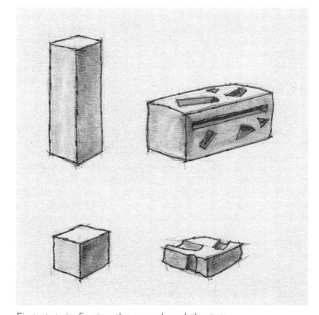

First step in forging the vessel and the top.

Vessel with lid in place.

the vessel. It took about five heats to force the ram to the desired depth. In this case the ram was taken down to within 1/4-inch of the bottom. The vessel was then placed in the slack tub to cool.

The top was then forged from a 2 inch cube of the same stock. It was hammered to a thickness of 1 1/2-inch and decorated and incised in the same manner as the vessel.

The tooling in the flypress was changed from the ram to a flat plate. The cool vessel was centered in the press and the red hot lid was placed on the top of the vessel; the plate was gently lowered and it flattened the lid into the vessel—two heats.

After cooling, the pieces were shot blasted to remove a very heavy deposit of scale. The shot blasting did not damage the surface of the metal, it brought out the quality of the surface of the splitting and tearing that the surface of the metal as the ram is forcing the vessel open. Polished with emory cloth, the part was finished with the wax and linseed oil mixture.

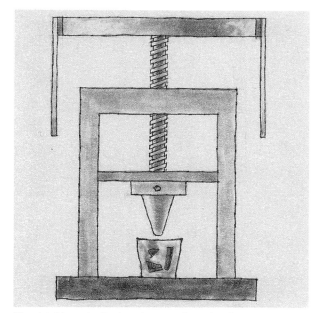

The third heat in forging the vessel on the flypress.

Enrique Vega
E. Vega Studios

Horizontal Sun Dial in the Westown Mall, Knoxville, TN, forged steel, brass and etched glass, 1994.

Enrique Vega has his metal working shop in Apex, North Carolina. He has been creating metalwork since 1980. Vega's architectural & public artwork includes custom railings, stairs, and gates, as well as furnishings and art pieces. Enrique takes a hands-on approach to his craft, from project development and computer design through actual creation and installation of the artwork. He describes his manner of working with the computer in the design and creation of his projects:

"To many artists the thought of using a computer in any phase of their artwork generates responses ranging from feeling intimidated by learning to use one, to skepticism that the computer may undermine the integrity of the work by stifling the human element of the design. But with the availability of graphics, video, and desktop publishing software, the personal computer today offers sophisticated tools that can help the designer create, track, and market his designs. The ability to reuse your designs in a variety of formats, makes working on a computer a valuable asset.

"The process of brainstorming or creating the design is first accomplished with plain paper and pencil. This is the critical point. If you don't have an idea, you can't make it better on the computer. Using a sketch pad, start with a very rough, but scaled renditions of the commission.

"The hand drawn artwork is then scanned into the computer. A scanner is an apparatus that digitizes an image and stores it on the computer hard disk. The scanned image is used as a template to visually aid in re-tracing the sketches.

"The abilities to cut, paste, duplicate, and resize objects a are the greatest advantages of computerizing the design process. From creating one leaf, copying it, pasting it, rotating it, resizing it, to scaling the design to full scale and outputting it to a continuous feed printer; the computerized illustration has ultimately saved many hours of repetitive work.

"The final layout process consists taping the image tiles together and tracing it using white tracing paper. This leaves a fine line tracing of the image on the work table.

"You can also send work-in-progress as faxes. With the properly equipped computer and video camera, you can quickly communicate to people all over the world! Take a video shot, plug it into the computer, and snap a picture of it. Dither it to the correct resolution, and output it to facsimiles, printers, or put it out into Cyberspace!

"The next time you get a request for information about your work, consider investing in a computer and desktop publishing software. No one will think you are a computer geek. Recognize that, just as you will spend years learning the art of blacksmithing, you will also have to devote time to learn this new technology. But, in the long run you will save money, create excellent presentations and keep esteemed clients up-to-date on your artwork.

In Enrique's work we go from the ancient sundial to cyberspace. An integration of time and space. I am not quite certain where it will all go—so make up your own mind and see "Internet" in the Resources section.

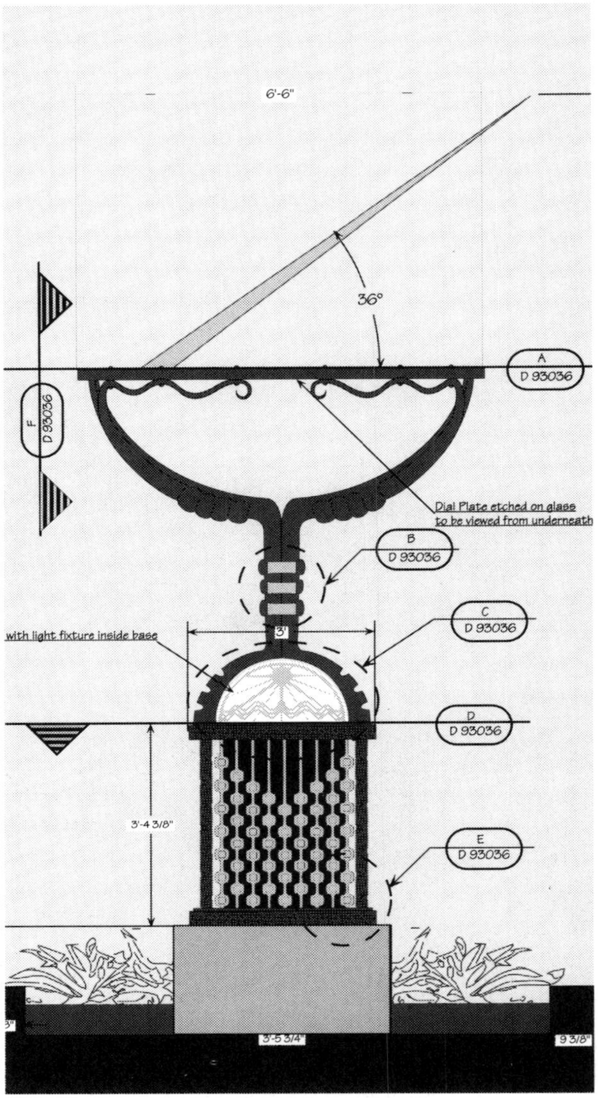

Computer drawing of the Horizontal Sun Dial.

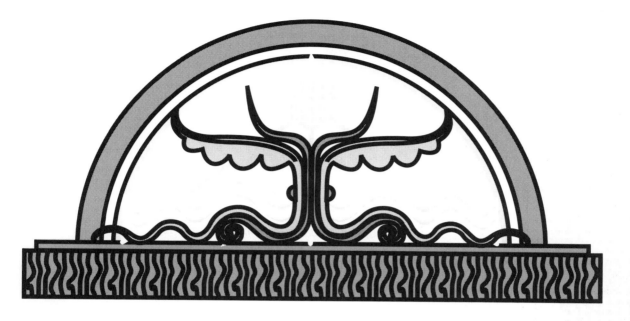

Computer drawing of Ethereal Light #1.

Ethereal Light #1, forged steel, brass, copper and etched glass, 1992. (Photo Michael Zirkle)

Design

There are a number of ways in which this section on visual design, setting up a business and business practices could be structured. My decision to place these topics under the umbrella of "Design" is influenced by my background and experience teaching in the field of industrial design for 33 years. I have used the principles of design in many different ways for solving many different types of problems, and I have come to realize that in many unrelated fields that design is an process that is utilized. It is a problem solving activity along with being a tool for organizing, planning, action and creating form. Wether it be in engineering design, architectural design, interior design, tool design or in metal design, these processes all require a vision and design is an envisioning process. Design is considered a creative activity and there is no question in my mind that metalworking, forging and making objects in metal is a creative endeavor. I am suggesting that looking at this whole design process from a different angle may make it easier to understand, less intimidating and encourage design to be used freely. With this in mind, let's approach design with an open and creative mind.

Rationale for Design/Business Planning

Although your immediate concerns have been setting up a forge and learning the forging processes, you may have notions of producing iron work for sale or of working in metals full time. If either is the case then you should consider planning a business, or in other words *designing* a business.

Some would say that the manner in which you manage your business is not a critical issue—that making iron is more important. If just forging iron is the central factor in your business, I would consider this a plan to *lose money* and have fun. I personally would prefer to *make money* and fun, and there are many examples of businesses in this category today. I believe the iron artistry and business acumen of Samuel Yellin are a testament, from the past, that both have been done with a superb standard. Going one step further, I would say in Yellin's case that one was not possible without the other. (See *Samuel Yellin, Metalworkers* in the "Bibliography," Resources.)

In the contemporary world there are a multitude of examples of artist/blacksmiths with well-managed and designed businesses. There are also a great number that could be doing much better if they were better organized and or designed. Several smiths that have formalized how to organize business are Don Plummer, a blacksmith and business consultant and Walter Scadden, an architectural blacksmith. They give lectures and write on the subject, and I have used some of their information which is brought together to make a working model—to design.

The elements of this design model are:
• Organization of your business, workshop or studio
• Project organization
• Approaches to visual design
• Use of the computer in planning and design
• The required action to do it!

The first step in any type of endeavor is making a conscious decision to commit to doing the task. This involves creating images about the type of activity you will be doing and how you will be doing it. You will have to run through several scenarios about your activities, your place of work, the type of iron you will be making and how you will be marketing and selling it. This can be a highly creative step, and you should devote some serious time to exploring a wide range of approaches and a diverse group of products. In other words, you must develop a "Vision." Approaching this exercise as a group can create a more dynamic group of scenarios. Our study will be restricted to individuals.

The creative day-dreaming can also include how you intend to go about manifesting these visions. This is the opportunity to begin to ask questions: How do I do this? What should I study? Who do I talk to? When should I start? Where am I to do all of this? What do I make? By asking and studying these questions you will begin to develop a "Strategy" to solve the issues raised. With this strategy you will begin to answer the questions and identify proper solutions.

If you have been trying to keep all of the mind-wandering and ideas in your head you may have lost some valuable information. This all should be recorded in a note-book or journal—you are collecting design information. In this process you will begin to answer these questions as you record the information and thus you have been identifying your "Objectives." Now it is time to do the first formal part of your planning: writing a plan—your plan of action. This is usually called your "Business Plan" and is an essential formal planning function that describes your business, your reasonable expectations, and the original intentions of how you will accomplish these objectives.

Below is a possible one year plan for a starting metalworker.

One Year Plan

Vision

I see myself setting up a forge behind my house where I will be learning basic forging techniques. I will explore several different metalworking areas to begin with. By the end of year I will select one of those to specialize in and devote full time energy to that area.

Strategies

I will build a shop and equip it with the basic tools.

I will get as much training and read as much as I can find available.

I will be as open to new areas as possible.

Objectives

Join ABANA and the local metals organization to meet as many people as possible.

Purchase books and magazines.

Have the building closed in during the first month.

Set up the forge and have it operating in the second month.

Attend a week long class during the third month.

After the plan is created the financial foundation must be laid; it is the working "Budget." This essential step gets one off to operating a successful business. The difference between the budget and planning, is the budget is the actual record of expenditures to compare against what you have planned. This is the financial road map which can tell you where you have been and compare this against where you are going.

First Year's Budget

Materials for building	$3,500.
Blacksmithing equipment, power tools	1,500.
Hand tools, safety equipment	400.
Miscellaneous supplies(coal, steel, etc.)	350.
Dues, training and travel	835.

To make all of this planning and budgeting meaningful, you must know how productive you are. We would all like to think that 100% of our work time is productive, however, this is not the case. In order to figure out accurate productivity, you must keep daily shop records of the time spent on various tasks. From this information you can begin to calculate your shop rates, material cost, profits, design costs and labor costs, which are necessary to develop the cost of a project, and critical to know before giving quotes. If you know these elements you can give a quote with a high degree of confidence. Much of these costs are based on the information gained by keeping accurate "Shop Records." The "Daily Shop Log," kept on 3 x 5 index cards, is one of the important parts of your records. Later these cards can be compiled, an area where the computer can certainly be a great tool. There are many inexpensive business programs that are a great help in compiling this type of information.

Daily Shop Log		March 4	
Activity	Time	Materials	Income
Build swage block stand	3	$12.00	
Practice making rivets	2	3.00	
Made 16 large spikes for builder	4	5.00	$80.00
Drawings of hooks for builder	1		
Totals	**10**	**$18.00**	**$80.00**

By keeping records over a period of a year you will have information to establish what your costs are and how much of your time is productive. If you have calculated the items above, the question, "What does it cost to make and how much should I charge?" is easily answered. If all of the aspects above have been addressed properly, you will know the costs of operating a business. Without this information you will only be guessing.

The next planning step is taking this information and projecting it out for two or three years. This can now be done with a great deal more confidence than previously.

"Marketing and Promotion" are elements that are critical in the development of a business. A good product is great, but it is not enough. You must develop an image of yourself and what your business is and then promote it. Time must be set aside for the proper development of a portfolio, business stationery, sales brochures and a general plan to market and sell your work.

"Confidence" is the last step but still an important building block in establishing a business. It is a function of life that allows you to proceed with a clear notion of who we are and how you wish to work.

One tool which can be a great benefit in helping you to keep an efficient system going is the computer. Today the cost of a computer system is reasonable and the new applications are easy to learn. A program that is in wide use to keep financial records is "Quicken." A more complex program for doing extensive spreadsheets is "Excel." There are also integrated packages combining several programs into one—spreadsheets, word processing, a data base, graphics and communications—which may also work for you.

Although it is beyond the scope of this book to explain all of the tools in depth and the mechanics of operating a business, one aspect that I stress is to start and continue your blacksmithing business in an orderly way. (If your approach to metalworking is part-time and casual, you will not need to be overly organized, but you will still have to design some things.) With the above information in place and your studio/workshop operating, it is time to examine the next function of an organized business. I call this is the "Design Method," others call it the "Project Life Cycle." Names are not important, what is, however, is that you begin to *recognize the value of planning on a regular basis.*

Design Method

Clearly stated by Charles Eames, one of America's greatest industrial designers, "design is a method of action." Design is the process of organizing your ideas, thoughts, plans, directions and visuals for a project, and acting on those aspects. It is not a mysterious process and can be broken down into a number of action phases. Normally there are six stages in a project, though each step is not always used fully in the design of the project.

1. The "Initial Step" is that time in which you accept the job to do a task. It could be as simple as saying, "Yes, I will make that grille for you." Or it could be challenging yourself with creating a new method of perfecting an old blacksmithing technique. This is also called the "Feasibility Step" where you survey yourself along with the time and resources needed to complete the job.

2. The "Analysis Step" involves collecting the information about the task. It could be probing the client for their preferences about wrought iron as well as taking the dimensions for the grille. Or perhaps you begin to collect all the information you can on the ways about the technique to be explored. The important aspect of this step, which can also be called the "Requirements Definition," is to gather all of the requirements for the work.

3. The "Idea Step" begins when you start making idea sketches and measured drawings for the project. It is the first step in which concrete ideas about the project begin to take shape. It could be making test samples or trying new tools and materials to expand on the original method. During the idea stage there are frequently times when you must go back to the previous stage for more information, clarification or to establish a new direction. This is the "Visual Design" step in which many ideas are created and elaborated upon. It is vital to this step to create and visualize as many ideas as possible, since a part of this phase is to evaluate those ideas and pick a direction with which to proceed. It requires a critical eye and mind for you (and /or the client) to discern the best elements and say, "This is the it."

4. In the "Forging" or "Production Step" much of the creative design work has been done, and the production planning and manufacture of the work can be implemented. It must be emphasized that during this time there is usually still a great deal of creative work done, for it is not until the heat of the fire that the idea can be truly realized. For most metal workers this is the most enjoyable step, made even more enjoyable especially when the planning is done, relieving much of the stress of uncertainty.

5. The "Installation" or "Implementation Step" is fine tuning with all of the final aspects being completed. In the case of the grille it would be the installation. In the case of the new forging technique, it would be actually using it.

6. The last stage is one which is frequently omitted or under valued; it is the time for critical analysis of one's work and of how and whether that work accomplishes its design goals. This is the time for introspection and "Evaluation" of the steps of your work. Don't forget to update your records, photograph your work and file the drawings.

A Note on Creativity

Everyone at times has blocks to being creative. We get our minds "locked up" and find it difficult to create new ideas or find new sources of inspiration. Sometimes it is best just to get away from the problem and come back later. Relax and look at things around you. A great book to read on the topic of breaking through the creative blocks is Roger Van Oech's, "A Whack on the Side of the Head: How You Can Be More Creative." This is also published as a computer program and as a deck of cards.

Approaching Metal Design

The formal aspects of design, such as the control and organization of line, plane, volume, shape, space, color and texture are important. If you have art or design training, it can be used to good advantage. If not, art or design courses will give you the formal knowledge that will enable you to design and analyze your work. But don't feel that you can't design just because you have not been to art school. You can, since everyone does it daily in many areas of their life. It is vital to realize that there are many different ways to approach design. By picking a method and applying your creative talents and by organizing the work in a meaningful way—you design.

Forging hot metal, with the given tools at one's disposal, is a strong and compelling force in directing the nature of what and how designs are created. It could be said that this is limiting and restrictive. But I strongly embrace both the past as well as what the "New Focus of Blacksmithing" will be. If chemical milling or use of a laser cutting machine or some new emerging technology brings on a new aspect to your designs, so be it.

"Change" is the force that brings entirely new answers to design. At times the scale in this approach is long and usually occurs in a closed culture. An example of the very long time scale is the evolution of the Plains Indian Tipi or the development of the European Cathedral. Each of these developments comes through the continually design improvements by many individuals over centuries and each reached a pinnacle in its design.

On the short time scale we have advances in technology which change rapidly: the development of the electronic tools and the multitude of these products that are being created today. In other cases a new material (plastics) or an industrial process (welding with the laser) has changed manufacturing of the basic materials, products and processes.

At times there is a functional reorganization of the parts of the product which brings about changes in how the product is used and how it looks, e.g., the redesign of the telephone from the wall hung crank model to the portable radio push-button phones. This process is moving at an extremely fast pace. Look around and notice the number of changes that are occurring in the arts and how metalworking is bringing about a new look.

Perhaps the most important influence on the design of wrought iron, because of its rich and long history, is the function of a "Historical Style." This approach to design uses the past to establish the style or character of the form. Designing a grille in the Art Deco style or an interior in the Gothic manner are examples of this approach. Usually this approach is directed by the client so that the style created will be in harmony with the existing style. If the project would be for the Washington Cathedral or the Federal Reserve Bank of New York, the design would be done as it was established many years ago. Samuel Yellin who created the work for both of these magnificent wrought iron masterpieces said about this approach to design;

The value to the craftsman does not lie in his opportunity to copy the old fragments in the museum, but rather he should so saturate his mind with a variety of designs in the medium with which he is familiar that he will learn to rely on is own judgment and instinctive sense of artistry in the execution of his own work.   [Samuel Yellin]

Yellin also used nature as a source for inspiration as many designers use natural forms as the source for ideas. The source is one that is always fresh, alive and ever changing. As an example, the acanthus leaf has been the classical natural motif used for centuries, used by artists and designers in every conceivable material. In using this approach one can be literal and use a leaf as it is picked off of a tree or use an abstraction of this leaf. One can also use the processes of nature and how things are formed, as might be the process of a climbing vine wrapping around a tree.

Self-expression is an individual's own way of approaching design. This artistic force simply expresses the need to create and to show expertise in a material or process or to express and idea which is important to that person. It is the expression of an idea or ideal. I feel that all artist/craftsmen express themselves in their work to some degree regardless of the type of work that they do. Is not dancing more important than "the dance?"

The use of a "Metaphor" is a method that provides a good approach to design. A metaphor can be physical forms or processes, words or myths, symbols or signs, ideas or ideals; these are elements to suggest a manner or new image in which to embody the design idea. As an example, consider the design of a window grille. Now think of the double breasted suit and how it overlaps the body, one side covering the other. Suppose your project at hand is to design a window grille. Imagine how the two sides might be opened for a clear view out of the window and then buttoned down. Visualize the effect of the overlapping sides coming together in the center. Imagine how this might be applied to a front door gate.

The most powerful factors affecting design will be the material, the tools used and the processes involved in forming the object. If the material and the forming processes are understood, designing and forging in iron will be expressed in their creation. These forces and processes will also be recognized and appreciated by the client or viewer. Yet the very nature of the power behind iron and forging is a limitation and hinders many in their discovery of the new. Break away by using "Analogies" from other processes. (Analogies are the resemblance of two things that are similar to one another.) Try to visualize techniques used by the woodworker (the use of dovetail joints), the tailor (stitching metals together), the bridge builder (by suspending objects from a cable) or a explosives engineer—the use of explosives to form metals was a creative leap into the unknown and now it is a process used in industry and in the creation of sculpture.

Draw to Get Started

An indispensable aspect of drawing for me has always been that, in the process of drawing, I am actually "drawing out" ideas from my inner being.

Just the physical act of making marks on paper starts the flow of ideas. It is as if these ideas are being created as they come out. It is a great feeling to see these new creations come to life.

A drawing session can be as important as a work session at the forge; true today as it was at the turn of the century when the following was written:

The young man who thinks of learning the blacksmith trade should first learn whether he is physically fitted for the peculiar labor. If satisfied on that point, he should immediately begin a course of study with special reference to the working of metals. He should also study freehand drawing. Every hour spent at the drawing board is an hour spent shaping irons, as he is training the hand to perform the work and the eye to see that it is true. And at no time should he drop the pencil. He should keep in mind the fact that the most skillful are the most successful. We do not mean skillful in one line only, but in all. The man who can direct, as well as execute, is the one who will make the greatest advancement, and to direct it is necessary to know why a thing should be done as well as how.　　　　[M. T. Richardson, *Practical Blacksmithing*, vol. III]

Drawing is a tool, as essential to the blacksmith as the hammer. Drawing gives form to ideas, just as the hammer gives form to the metal. If you try to forge without preparation, forging can be difficult. You may occasionally want to experiment at the forge. Great! But in general, it is a good idea to plan your work ahead of time. Try working for a whole day at the forge without any preparation or plan and see what happens and what doesn't happen.

From my experience it is apparent when starting a design project at the idea stage is the point at which many lock up their creative energy and just create one idea. Once started it is easier to generate many ideas. In this initial stage, I generally work with drawings, usually with small pencil sketches done on inexpensive onion skin paper. Most drawings are to a relative scale which helps me to understand what the proportions will be. My initial sketches are scaled at one inch equals one foot. After some time the scale aspect falls into place and you will find that you are drawing to scale. This works particularly well with architectural projects. At times I will use grid paper and this provides a structure and scale if these elements are required.

I also do design drawings in a sketchbook, usually an 8 1/2 x 11-inch wire-bound plain paper notebook. If I have an idea for a new piece of iron or a new way to work it, I draw it. I really enjoy this sketchbook because it is the place where I can give form to my ideas and have fun with them. First, I envision the complete piece and then I draw it to understand how it will be forged. This process is invaluable because many of my trials and errors have been on paper and not at the forge. This saves a lot of time.

There are several important aspects of drawing that I want to stress. First, anyone can draw and sketch, so just do it. Drawing well takes practice and experience and the more you draw, the better your drawings will be and the more fun you will have. Also, drawing is a form of communication. It is communication with yourself; as the idea develops and grows, a dialogue is set up between you and the drawing. When this works well it can be called interactive drawing and there really is a dialogue. Later this dialogue is with a colleague, client or architect. Drawings can then really tell a story. How good a story teller are you?

I work at my drawing table with onion skin paper; with this paper it is easy to do overlays of drawings and easily make changes and adjustments. I prefer to work with soft lead pencils with an eraser. The soft graphite in these pencils allows me to smudge the drawing to add depth. I use the eraser to "draw" in highlights, not to correct mistakes. These are my choices of material, but you should select the media that is the best for you.

There is a way to draw three-dimensionally, and that is by using clay (Plastaline, an oil based clay) as a sketch medium. You can give substance to your ideas by forming in clay those things that you would like to form later in iron at the forge. Clay is a good medium in which to practice while you are assembling your equipment and setting up your forge. For three-dimensional sheet metal projects, cutting out heavy kraft paper and joining with masking tape is quick a quick sketch material. Soft aluminum and copper wire make good sketch materials also.

Recently I have been using the computer more to do sketching and idea development. I believe it is because as I rewrite this book I am using the computer more and find that it is easier for me to sketch out an idea. Recently I started a new sketch book, a collection of computer drawings labeled, "Silicone Iron." It's been a long road from sketching in my journals in the tipi.

As a final note on drawing, several more aspects should be considered. It is vital to make a survey of the site when working on an architectural project. Accurate measurements are critical. Photographs are helpful since it is always difficult to remember all of the details. With the dimensions and details the next phase can be started, and that is placing your ideas in context. The type of drawing required for this is orthographic drawing or engineering drawing. These drawings are drawn to scale and use a widely known set of conventions and standards. There are a number of good text books for learning orthographic drawing available in the library. If you want to start with one book I would recommend *Draw,* by Hanks and Belliston.

Metal Design
and the Computer

Shortly after the first edition of this book was published in 1977, I purchased my first computer, an Osborne. I used it for word processing and record keeping. I was thrilled by the newly discovered power of this unique tool. Later when the Macintosh computer was introduced, I purchased one and was truly amazed at the Mac's broad power and versatility along with new applications for word processing, spreadsheets and graphics. The most important new dimension for me was the use of graphics. I started using the Mac for drawing and creating designs. In short order I found out that I could quickly do some types of design work more quickly and much easier with a greater range of ideas. The increased power, speed and number of applications for the computer continues and seemingly has no end..I found that it was an incredible tool to organize and planing business functions, and it was a wonderful visual design tool.

Before one should think about a computer for their business or design work they should set up a tenet which I have used, "Work smarter, not harder." If any task is going to be harder with the purchase of a new tool, then make the decision to work smarter with whatever tools you have at your disposal. Keep an alert eye for how the computer or any other tool can be useful in your work. Check with friends or another smith who has used a computer in his or her work to see how this tool may be useful for you.

Six examples of using a line drawing, show to the left, and repeating it twelve times about a center.

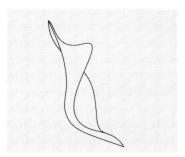

The line drawing for the pinwheel.

A few guidelines for making a decision to use the computer: if there are many repeat elements in the design, if there is the possibility that many changes are likely to be made, if speed and accuracy are a requirement, if keeping track of many elements in the project and if you really want to try an exciting experience.

As an example, how do you make a drawing of a circular motif of 12 elements, as you might do for a clock? The drawing of several variations may be made in just minutes by using the power duplicate function in the computer program Freehand. The six pinwheels sketches drawn on the previous page were done in about 20 minutes. For the clock face on this page, the sketch of the lines above took about 2 minutes, and then the 12 parts were duplicated and rotated in less then a minute.

The basic layout of a clock, or a 12 part figure, can also be done on paper with a "T" square and 30°- 60° triangle and a design traced 12 times. Can you do the same thing with a more complex design, such as a circular repeat of 18 elements rotated at 20° and then stretched. How long would it take?

Each of the techniques discovered with the computer can lead to completely new forms and ideas. The examples show on this and the previous pages I did for the first time, and I was just playing games. It opened up for me a new series of possibilities to explore. It is similar to any type of drawing experience where the objects and forms that are created become new images which create new

A pinwheel clock drawn with the computer program Freehand.

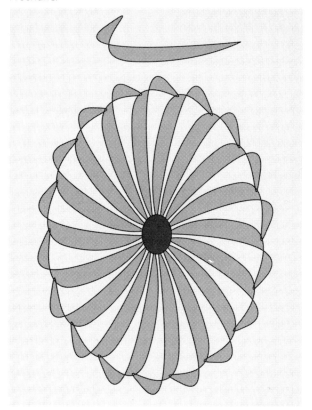

A stretched circular repeat of 18 elements in 20°steps.

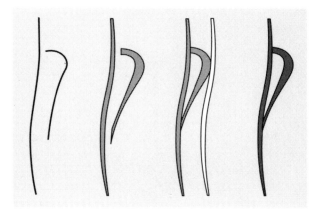

The two lines drawn and duplicated then placed together to form the balustrade.

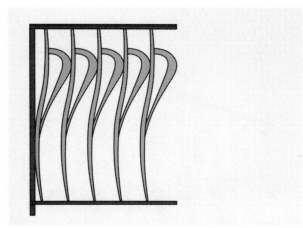

The balustrade repeated five times and placed in the frame.

directions. True the computer is not quite the same as using a pencil and paper, but if you begin to explore—you will find something new.

Multiple elements, such as a balustrade in a railing, can easily traced on paper, but with the computer it is faster to visualize different variations and much more accurate. For the design of the railing, on this page, the starting point is several curved lines. Repeat the lines and join them together, then fill with a grey to give the effect of solidity. Place a single line to the right to check on alignment and how they would be joined. Duplicate five units in line and frame with heavier support sections. Notice that one end is left open to take up the other support. With this basic module duplicate two more to make the railing. An end post is added to complete the rail. This module could be repeated as many times as necessary.

Duplicate of the rail and skew it at a 30°. The design is aligned as it might be seen on a staircase at a 30° angle. The original proportions remaining the same, however, the whole rail could be expanded or shortened to adjust to the length of the run. This is easily done by changing the vertical or horizontal proportions. In the case below, the railing is lengthened. The stair railing is on the next page.

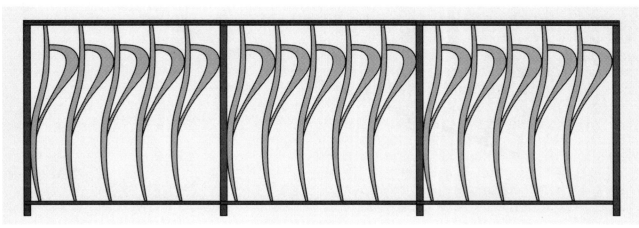

The basic module repeated three times and extend on the horizontal axis.

Many design projects use a basic motif or module which is used in different sizes, proportions, number, arrangement and position. (At times a copier may be used to enlarge and create many of the same modules.) The computer really shows it's versatility and power when you vary the proportion and the manner in which the elements are joined.

Draw a calligraphic pen stroke and fill with a grey, as show on the next page. Duplicate this stroke and invert it. (At this point I saw that that the image was one of split iron, and envisioned how it might be used in a grille.) Join the two strokes together and group them. Duplicate this basic unit horizontally four times and group them. Duplicate this new group three times vertically and place a frame to form the grille. Add collars for detail. (See page 238 for another version.)

From a graphic design standpoint, frequently you have drawn an object that you would like to use in a publication or a design and it is sometimes difficult to

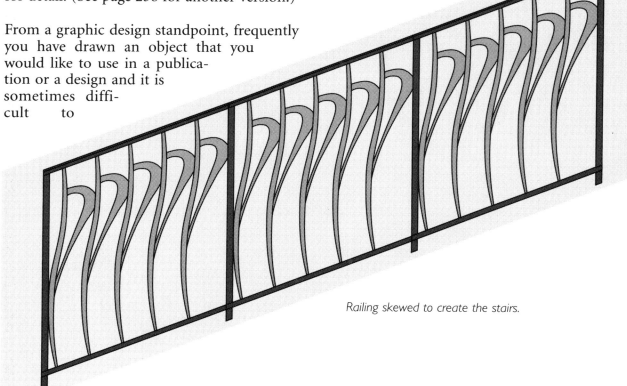

Railing skewed to create the stairs.

210

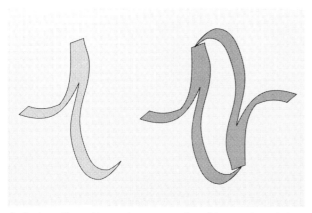

A single calligraphic stroke repeated and inverted, and the two pieces are joined together.

scale properly. There may be some changes that you would like to make to the design; if the information is digital, as in a computer, then it is easy to manipulate and print in many forms.

There are many CAD (computed aided drawing) programs which may be used to do orthographic drawings. For large complex projects CAD can be a big help. There is also the aspect of accuracy in complex projects; CAD excels here. The interesting aspect to each of these examples of computer drawings is that they are permanently digitally recorded and stored. Later these can be brought up on the computer screen and be used as the basis for new designs.

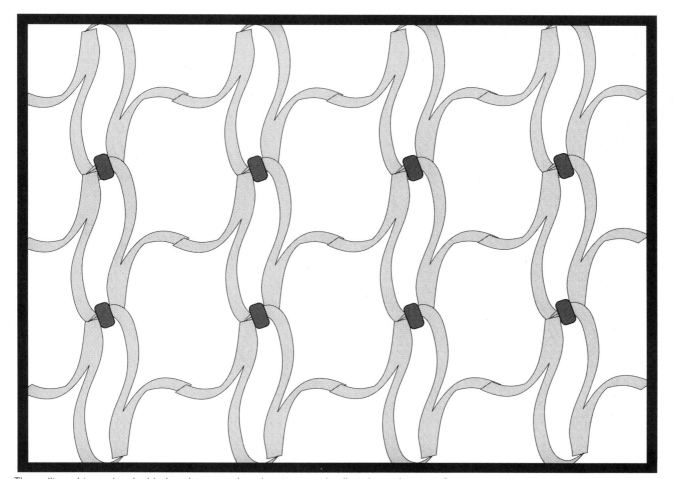

The calligraphic stroke doubled and repeated twelve times and collared together in a frame.

Resources

The Resources section is a collection of information, descriptions, addresses and charts, which may be useful to the metalworker. It is an eclectic assemblage of things which have been useful to others, and that utility is the basis for their selection.

Diameter	Circumference	Diameter	Circumference	Diameter	Circumference
1/4	0.7854	12	37.69	24 1/2	76.96
1/2	1.570	12 1/2	39.27	25	78.54
3/4	2.256	13	40.84	25 1/2	80.10
1	3.141	13 1/2	42.41	26	81.68
1 1/2	4.712	14	43.98	26 1/2	83.25
2	6.283	14 1/2	45.55	27	84.82
2 1/2	7.854	15	47.12	27 1/2	86.39
3	9.424	15 1/2	48.69	28	87.96
3 1/2	10.99	16	50.26	28 1/2	89.53
4	12.56	16 1/2	51.83	29	91.10
4 1/2	14.13	17	53.40	29 1/2	92.67
5	15.70	17 1/2	54.97	30	94.24
5 1/2	17.27	18	56.54	30 1/2	95.81
6	18.84	18 1/2	58.11	31	97.38
6 1/2	20.42	19	59.69	31 1/2	98.96
7	21.99	19 1/2	61.26	32	100.5
7 1/2	23.56	20	62.83	32 1/2	102.1
8	25.13	20 1/2	64.40	33	103.6
8 1/2	26.70	21	65.97	33 1/2	105.2
9	28.27	21 1/2	67.54	34	106.8
9 1/2	29.84	22	69.11	34 1/2	108.3
10	31.41	22 1/2	70.68	35	109.9
10 1/2	32.98	23	72.25	35 1/2	111.5
11	34.55	23 1/2	73.82	36	113.0
11 1/2	36.12	24	75.39		

Chart 10. Circumferences of circles in inches.

Abrasives and Sharpening

Many blacksmithing tools can be sharpened on a bench grinder or belt sander. When dressing tools after they have been forged, this is not a concern since they will be heat treated later. It is important to know what basic abrasive materials and their working properties if making bladed tools (knives, chisels or axes) for your own use or for resale.

Abrasives are classified by the materials they are made of and the grit or particle size of the material. There are many trade names for these stones, wheels, belts and papers, causing some confusion, so only the generic names are used here.

Silicone carbide is a hard, man-made material, dark gray in color, with the particles the shape of spikes of broken glass. Silicone carbide removes metal very fast, but does not develop a keen edge. Aluminum oxide is a man-made material, tan to white in color, with the shape of the particles being cubic, similar in shape to grains of sand. Aluminum oxide does not remove metal as fast as silicone carbide, but it develops a much keener edge. Noviculite is a natural stone, ranging in color from white to black, and is called "Arkansas stone." The Arkansas stones range from a soft coarse grit to the extremely hard fine grit. The choice of stones is a matter of personal preference and cost, but it is good to have at least 3 stones: coarse, medium and fine.

When using a stone, always use honing oil to flush away the particles of metal that is removed from the blade. If this is not done the stone can become clogged with metal particles and become ineffective. It is best not to use motor oil since it has additives which could gum up the stone. Use a honing oil or mineral oil and mix with equal measures of kerosene or paint thinner to thin the oil for best results. Always clean the stone with a cloth and oil after use.

The steps in sharpening a tool are: reshaping the tool and dressing the cutting edge with the coarse stone, refining the edge with a medium stone, the final sharpening with a fine stone and the last step of stropping the blade.

To sharpen the blade of the tool, flood the stone with oil, lay the blade on the stone and draw the blade back and forth across the entire length of the stone. It is not necessary to turn the tool over after each stroke. For a wedge-shaped flat blade, maintain a steady, firm pressure and do not rock the blade. For a blade that is slightly rounded, a slight circular motion is acceptable. Check for the desired shape of the blade surface by holding the blade under a strong light and moving it around to see if the entire blade has the same texture on it. If it does not, you are able to see where the blade has been on the stone since it has a dull finish. Grind both sides on this stone and move to the finer grades of stones. As each finer grade of abrasive is used, a more polished surface and the final shape of the blade is developed.

The final step is to strop the tool which removes any burr that developed. The strop polishes the edge and removes the burr to create a keen edge. The strop is made with a piece of hard belt leather attached to a piece of wood. It should be a minimum of 2 inches wide and at least 8 inches long. Coat the leather with a little oil and dust with aluminum oxide powder, 400 to 600 grit. It is the simplest piece of all the sharpening tools and the most neglected.

To test for sharpness hold the edge of the tool so that a strong light shines directly from above on the edge. Move it from side to side, and any nick or dull spots will reflect the light; if the tool is sharp there will be no reflected light along the edge. The final test for sharpness is to make a cut. A properly sharpened bladed tool cuts smoothly and easily. Remember that a sharp tool is much safer to use, since there is less effort required to make the cut.

Diameter of Drill	Soft Metals 300 F.P.M.	Plastics and Hard Rubber 200 F.P.M.	Mild Steel 100 F.P.M.	Hard Cast Iron 80 F.P.M.	Tool or Hard Steel 60 F.P.M.
1/16 (No. 53 to 80)	18320	12217	6111	4889	3667
3/32 (No. 42 to 52)	12212	8142	4071	3258	2442
1/8 (No. 31 to 41)	9160	6112	3056	2445	1833
5/32 (No. 23 to 30)	7328	4888	2444	1954	1465
3/16 (No. 13 to 22)	6106	4075	2037	1630	1222
7/32 (No. 1 to 12)	5234	3490	1745	1396	1047
1/4 (A to E)	4575	3055	1527	1222	917
9/32 (G to K)	4071	2712	1356	1084	814
5/16 (L, M, N)	3660	2445	1222	978	733
11/32 (O to R)	3330	2220	1110	888	666
3/8 (S, T, U)	3050	2037	1018	815	611
13/32 (V to Z)	2818	1878	939	752	563
7/16	2614	1746	873	698	524
15/32	2442	1628	814	652	488
1/2	2287	1528	764	611	458
9/16	2035	1357	678	543	407
5/8	1830	1222	611	489	367
11/16	1665	1110	555	444	333
3/4	1525	1018	509	407	306

Figures are for High-Speed Drills. The speed of Carbide Drills should be reduced by one-half. Use drill speed nearest to figure given.

Chart 11. Drill speeds in R.P.M.

Fraction	Decimal	Millimeters	Fraction	Decimal	Millimeters
1/64	.015625	0.39688	33/64	.515625	13.09690
1/32	.03125	0.79375	17/32	.53125	13.49378
3/64	.046875	1.19063	35/64	.546875	13.89065
1/16	.0625	1.58750	9/16	.5625	14.28753
5/64	.078125	1.98438	37/64	.578125	14.68440
3/32	.09375	2.38125	19/32	.59375	15.08128
7/64	.109375	2.77813	39/64	.609375	15.47816
1/8	.125	3.17501	5/8	.625	15.87503
9/64	.140625	3.57188	41/64	.640625	16.27191
5/32	.15625	3.96876	21/32	.65625	16.66878
11/64	.171875	4.36563	43/64	.671875	17.06566
3/16	.1875	4.76251	11/16	.6875	17.46253
13/64	.203125	5.15939	45/64	.703125	17.85941
7/32	.21875	5.55626	23/32	.71875	18.25629
15/64	.234375	5.95314	47/64	.734375	18.65316
1/4	.25	6.35001	3/4	.75	19.05004
17/64	.265625	6.74689	49/64	.765625	19.44691
9/32	.28125	7.14376	25/32	.78125	19.84379
19/64	.296875	7.54064	51/64	.796875	20.03442
5/16	.3125	7.93752	13/16	.8125	20.63754
21/64	.328125	8.33439	53/64	.828125	21.03442
11/32	.34375	8.73127	27/32	.84375	21.43129
23/64	.359375	9.12814	55/64	.859375	21.82817
3/8	.375	9.52502	7/8	.875	22.22504
25/64	.390625	9.92189	57/64	.890625	22.62192
13/32	.40625	10.31877	29/32	.90625	23.01880
27/64	.421875	10.71565	59/64	.921875	23.41567
7/16	.4375	11.11252	15/16	.9375	23.81255
29/64	.453125	11.50940	61/64	.953125	24.20942
15/32	.46875	11.90627	31/32	.96875	24.60630
31/64	.484375	12.30315	63/64	.984375	25.00318
1/2	.5	12.70003	1	1.	25.40005

Chart 12. Inch–millimeter decimal equivalents.

Size	Rounds		Squares		Hexagons		Octagons	
	Per Ft.	Per In.	Per Ft.	Per In.	Per Ft.	Per In.	Per Ft.	Per In.
1/8	.042	.004	.053	.004	.046	.004	.044	.004
3/16	.094	.008	.120	.010	.104	.009	.099	.008
1/4	.167	.014	.213	.018	.184	.015	.176	.015
5/16	.261	.022	.332	.028	.288	.024	.275	.023
3/8	.376	.031	.478	.040	.414	.035	.396	.033
7/16	.511	.043	.651	.054	.564	.047	.539	.045
1/2	.688	.056	.850	.071	.737	.061	.704	.059
9/16	.854	.070	1.076	.090	.932	.078	.891	.074
5/8	1.040	.087	1.328	.111	1.150	.096	1.100	.092
11/16	1.260	.105	1.607	.134	1.393	.116	1.331	.111
3/4	1.500	.125	1.913	.159	1.658	.138	1.584	.132
13/16	1.760	.147	2.245	.187	1.944	.162	1.859	.155
7/8	2.040	.170	2.603	.217	2.256	.188	2.157	.180
15/16	2.350	.196	2.988	.249	2.588	.216	2.476	.206
1	2.670	.223	3.400	.283	2.944	.245	2.817	.235
1 1/16	3.010	.251	3.838	.320	3.324	.277	3.180	.265
1 1/8	3.380	.282	4.303	.359	3.727	.311	3.565	.297
1 3/16	3.770	.314	4.795	.400	4.152	.346	3.972	.331
1 1/4	4.170	.348	5.314	.443	4.601	.383	4.401	.367
1 5/16	4.600	.383	5.857	.488	5.072	.423	4.852	.404
1 3/8	5.050	.421	6.428	.536	5.567	.464	5.325	.444
1 7/16	5.517	.460	7.026	.586	6.085	.507	5.820	.485
1 1/2	6.010	.501	7.650	.638	6.625	.552	6.338	.528
1 9/16	6.519	.543	8.301	.692	7.189	.559	6.877	.573
1 5/8	7.050	.588	8.978	.748	7.775	.648	7.438	.620
1 11/16	7.604	.634	9.682	.807	8.385	.699	8.021	.668
1 3/4	8.180	.682	10.414	.868	9.018	.752	8.626	.719
1 13/16	8.773	.731	11.170	.931	9.673	.806	9.253	.771
1 7/8	9.390	.783	12.000	1.000	10.355	.863	9.902	.825
1 15/16	10.024	.835	12.763	1.064	11.053	.921	10.574	.881
2	10.700	.892	13.600	1.133	11.780	.982	11.267	.939
2 1/16	11.360	.947	14.463	1.205	12.528	1.044	11.982	.999
2 1/8	12.058	1.005	15.354	1.280	13.300	1.108	12.719	1.060
2 3/16	12.778	1.065	16.270	1.355	14.092	1.174	13.478	1.123
2 1/4	13.519	1.127	17.213	1.434	14.911	1.243	14.259	1.188
2 5/16	14.280	1.190	18.182	1.515	15.747	1.312	15.063	1.255
2 3/8	15.063	1.255	19.178	1.598	16.613	1.384	15.888	1.324
2 7/16	15.866	1.322	20.201	1.683	17.496	1.458	16.735	1.395
2 1/2	16.690	1.391	21.250	1.771	18.403	1.534	17.604	1.467

Chart 13. Weight of mild steel bars.

Width (inches)	Thickness (inches)											
	1/16	1/8	3/16	1/4	5/16	3/8	7/16	1/2	5/8	3/4	7/8	1
1/4	.053	.106	.159	.213	.266	.319	.372	.425	.531	.638	.744	.850
1/2	.106	.213	.319	.425	.531	.638	.744	.850	1.063	1.275	1.488	1.700
3/4	.159	.319	.478	.638	.797	.956	1.116	1.275	1.594	1.913	2.231	2.550
1	.213	.425	.638	.850	1.063	1.275	1.488	1.700	2.125	2.550	2.975	3.400
1 1/4	.266	.531	.797	1.063	1.328	1.594	1.859	2.125	2.656	3.188	3.719	4.250
1 1/2	.319	.638	.956	1.275	1.594	2.913	2.231	2.550	3.188	3.825	4.463	5.100
1 3/4	.372	.744	1.116	1.488	1.859	2.231	2.603	2.975	3.719	4.463	5.206	5.950
2	.425	.850	1.275	1.700	2.125	2.550	2.975	3.400	4.250	5.100	5.950	6.800
2 1/4	.478	.956	1.434	1.913	2.391	2.869	3.347	3.825	4.781	5.738	6.694	7.650
2 1/2	.531	1.063	1.594	2.125	2.656	3.188	3.719	4.250	5.313	6.375	7.438	8.500
2 3/4	.584	1.169	1.753	2.338	2.922	3.506	4.091	4.675	5.844	7.013	8.181	9.350
3	.638	1.275	1.913	2.550	3.188	3.825	4.463	5.100	6.375	7.650	8.925	10.20
3 1/4	.691	1.381	2.072	2.736	3.453	4.144	4.834	5.525	6.906	8.288	9.669	11.05
3 1/2	.744	1.488	2.231	2.975	3.719	4.463	5.206	5.950	7.438	8.925	10.41	11.90
3 3/4	.797	1.594	2.391	3.188	3.984	4.781	5.578	6.375	7.969	9.563	11.16	12.75
4	.850	1.700	2.550	3.400	4.250	5.100	5.950	6.800	8.500	10.20	11.90	13.60
4 1/4	.903	1.806	2.709	3.613	4.516	5.419	6.322	7.225	9.031	10.84	12.64	14.45
4 1/2	.956	1.913	2.869	3.825	4.781	5.738	6.694	7.650	9.563	11.48	13.39	15.30
4 3/4	1.009	2.019	3.028	4.038	5.047	6.056	7.066	8.075	10.09	12.11	14.13	16.15
5	1.063	2.125	3.188	4.250	5.313	6.375	7.438	8.500	10.63	12.75	14.88	17.00

Chart 14. Weight of square edge mild steel bars.

Gas Torches

The basic propane gas torch is simple, is readily available and is an inexpensive source of heat. It comes in a variety of sizes and needs little training to use. Use it for soldering, brazing and small heating tasks.

The oxy-acetylene torch, because of its higher heat, is useful for a wide variety of tasks. The basis of this unit is a torch connected by hoses and regulators to a tank of compressed oxygen and compressed acetylene. When these two gases are mixed in the torch and ignited, they create an extremely hot flame. This can be used to solder, braze, weld and flame-cut a variety of metals. One of the more useful tasks for the gas torch blacksmith is to concentrate heat at a specific area, such as a rivet head, a bar to be bent or a piece to be adjusted. Since an oxy-acetylene rig is portable, it is easy to carry on location and is a good source of heat to do installations and repair work.

There are other gases that can be used instead of acetylene. Generally, they will be cheaper but not as hot as acetylene. Check with you local supplier to see what is available.

Gas Welding and Arc Welding

Bronze-welding or brazing is joining metals with bronze-welding rods. It is stronger than silver solder and can be used to weld cast iron, steel and other metals. With this type of weld, the rod material (bronze) is melted onto the part and will be noticeable on steel because of the difference in the metal colors; this can be used to advantage if desired. Fluxes are used with brazing.

Welding steel with steel welding rods gives the stronger weld than brazing and can be finished off to the same color as the steel. It joins the pieces by melting both the rod and the parts being welded. Small steel pieces and sheet metals are easily welded with gas, but is difficult for large and thicker parts.

Arc welding uses an electrical current of low voltage and high amperage to melt an electrode and the parts to be joined. Arc welding can be used on any size or thickness of steel and many other metals. This type of weld gives the strongest most serviceable of the welds. There are a number of different types of arc welding systems. The most common is the use of a coated welding rod, usually called "stick welding." More complex systems are shielded metal-arc welding systems which use inert gases around the weld area. This prevents the weld from being contaminated by oxidation, scale and other impurities.

One of the important qualities of arc welding is that it is used to repair the face and edges of anvils and other tools. This requires special welding rods and skills, but damaged tools and equipment can be made serviceable by these repairs.

A word of caution when working with welding materials. When heated, metals, welding rods, plated or coated metals and fluxes give off gases that are harmful and can cause illness. Be extremely careful to use good shop sense and properly ventilate your forge. Welding can be a dangerous activity and you should not attempt to use this type of equipment without proper training. Take classes or work with a trained welder.

Steel Used in General Motors Cars and Trucks	
Leaf Spring	5160
Coil Spring	5160 or 9260
Axle Shaft	1050
Transmission Shaft	1141
Inlet Engine Valve	3140
Exhaust Engine Valve	Armco #21-4N
Connecting Rod	1038 or 10374

Chart 15. Steel used in older GM cars and trucks.

Soldering

There are two types of soldering which do not melt the metals to be joined, but melt metals to join the pieces together. Soft soldering uses metal alloys that melt between 350° F and 700°F. The soft solders are alloys of lead and tin; 50% lead and 50% tin is the most commonly used alloy and melts at 361°F. Other soft solders have varying percentages of these metals along with cadmium and antimony. Do not use an alloy that has lead in it; use only pure tin when soldering utensils to be used around food. Hard soldering (frequently called silver-soldering) uses metal alloys that melt between 1100°F and 1500°F. The hard solder alloys are composed of silver, copper, zinc and cadmium in varying percentages. An alloy of 65% silver, 20% copper and 15% melts at 1280°F. Fluxes for both types of solder are required. A propane torch can be used for soldering and is fine for small objects where an oxy-acetylene torch would be to hot.

No.	Size	No.	Size	No.	Size	Letter	Size
80	0.0135	53	0.0595	26	0.1470	A	0.2340
79	0.0145	52	0.0635	25	0.1495	B	0.2380
78	0.0160	51	0.0670	24	0.1520	C	0.2420
77	0.0180	50	0.0700	23	0.1540	D	0.2460
76	0.0200	49	0.0730	22	0.1570	E	0.2500
75	0.0210	48	0.0760	21	0.1590	F	0.2570
74	0.0225	47	0.0785	20	0.1610	G	0.2610
73	0.0240	46	0.0810	19	0.1660	H	0.2660
72	0.0250	45	0.0820	18	0.1695	I	0.2720
71	0.0260	44	0.0860	17	0.1730	J	0.2770
70	0.0280	43	0.0890	16	0.1770	K	0.2810
69	0.0292	42	0.0935	15	0.1800	L	0.2900
68	0.0310	41	0.0960	14	0.1820	M	0.2950
67	0.0320	40	0.0980	13	0.1850	N	0.3020
66	0.0330	39	0.0995	12	0.1890	O	0.3160
65	0.0350	38	0.1015	11	0.1910	P	0.3230
64	0.0360	37	0.1040	10	0.1935	Q	0.3320
63	0.0370	36	0.1065	9	0.1960	R	0.3390
62	0.0380	35	0.1100	8	0.1990	S	0.3480
61	0.0390	34	0.1110	7	0.2010	T	0.3580
60	0.0400	33	0.1130	6	0.2040	U	0.3680
59	0.0410	32	0.1160	5	0.2055	V	0.3770
58	0.0420	31	0.1200	4	0.2090	W	0.3860
57	0.0430	30	0.1285	3	0.2130	X	0.3970
56	0.0465	29	0.1360	2	0.2210	Y	0.4040
55	0.0520	28	0.1405	1	0.2280	Z	0.4130
54	0.0550	27	0.1440				

Chart 16. Sizes of numbered and lettered drills.

Magazines (also see organizations)

Anvil Magazine
PO Box 1810
Georgetown, CA 95634-1810

A farriers journal with articles on smithing

916-333-2142

Hephaistos
Internationale Zeitschrift für Metallgestalter
Kirchplatz 8
D-82538 Geretsreid, Germany

An international blacksmithing journal

The Crafts Report, The Business Journal for the Craft Industry. (The name says it.)
300 Water St.
PO Box 1992
Wilmington, DE 19899

302-656-2209

Blacksmith Journal
Rt 1 Box 189
Lonedell, MO 63060

Monthly supplements of smithing techniques

314-629-4061

Buffing

Buffing gets it name from the wheels fixed to a polishing head or an arbor of an electric motor. Abrasives are applied to the spinning buffs and the parts polished. This refines the metal's surface to a bright shiny finish. When buffing softer metals aluminum, brass and copper—tripoli, crocus and rouge is used. Tripoli is decomposed limestone and is used for rough polishing. Crocus and rouge are iron oxide and are used for the finishing polish. When buffing steel the same basic materials are used as in sharpening. For buffing steel varying grades of silicone carbide are used to rough the piece and then finished with either aluminum oxide or rouge.

These compounds are mixed with waxes and cast into bars or tubes that are easily applied to the rotating buffs. Buffs are generally made of cotton cloth sewn together, however, felt and leather are also used. Another type of buff is a wheel made of nylon fibers bound together with the abrasive fused into the fibers. They are made in three grits: fine, medium and coarse. This type of wheel is slightly flexible and is limitated for polishing small and delicate surfaces, but is a really wonderful polishing tool.

Buffing with power equipment is definitely easier than doing it by hand, however there are two things to be aware of. The first is that a spinning buff or fiber wheel easily grabs the piece and throw it, so you must be careful not to force the piece into the wheel too aggressively. Also, watch out for ends, edges or corners to catch in the wheel. The second is that mechanical finishing gives the surface of the piece a look of sameness; that is, all of the polish marks are going in the same direction. If that is what you want, fine. If not, finish it off by hand for a more random look.

Spark Test

If you do not know the exact nature of a metal, the simplest way to identify it is to examine the color, weight and surface finish. As you gain experience, this will become easier. A test for magnetism will help you identify iron-based metals, particularly if they have been plated or painted. This test can also be used to sort out the 400 series of stainless steels, which are magnetic, from the 300 series, which are non-magnetic.

This visual examination, however, has its limits and tells you nothing about the basic content of the metal. For all ferrous alloys the best shop method is to use the spark test. This test does not work on most non-ferrous metals.

You can use the spark test to sort out the general types of steel, to determine the approximate amount of carbon in steel and sometimes, to pinpoint the general type of alloy steel. To make this test, grind the test piece on the bench grinder, and observe the stream of sparks. You should make this test under carefully controlled conditions: first put on your safety glasses and stand in the same position, making sure that your line of view is perpendicular to the stream of sparks. Each time you do this test, make sure that the lighting in the shop is the same and make sure that you exert the same amount of pressure as you hold each piece against the grinding wheel. (If you increase the pressure against the wheel, the temperature of the spark stream will be raised, changing its appearance.) Look for the color of the sparks, the length and amount of the stream, the streaks or leaders, the nature of the bursts or stars and the amount of feathering. Try this test on pieces of known steel. Use these identified pieces as controls as you learn this technique. It takes experience and practice. Refer to Chart 14 and notice that, as the carbon content is increased, the bursts increase and the stream shortens. This is because greater concentrations of carbon burn more rapidly. Also, carbon in the alloy gives the stream of sparks a distinct reddish color. In contrast, high-speed steel is more of an orange yellow. Each alloy will change the color slightly.

Label these pieces of known metal and hang them up behind your bench grinder.

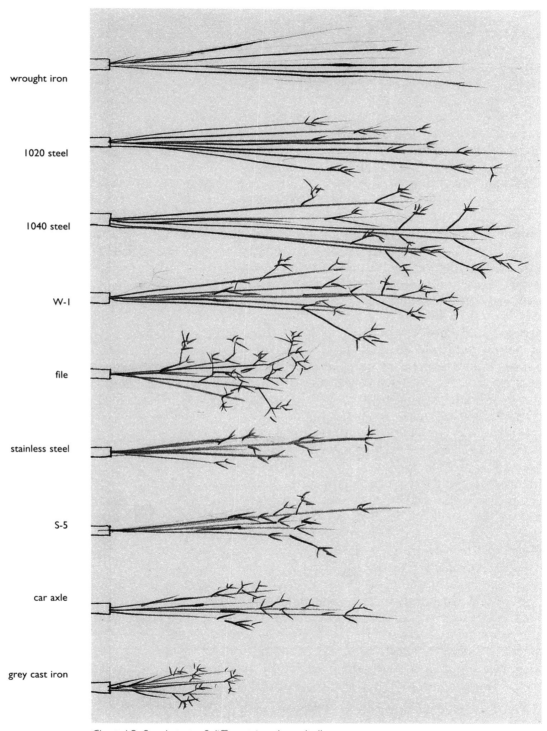

wrought iron

1020 steel

1040 steel

W-1

file

stainless steel

S-5

car axle

grey cast iron

Chart 18. Spark test of different iron based alloys.

Forging Nonferrous Metals

Generally, alloys of copper and tin are called "bronze" and alloys of copper and zinc are called "brass." Through use, the terms have almost become interchangeable. There is a numbering system for these metals and more information can be obtained from the Copper Development Association, Greenwich, CT.

Copper and copper alloys can be forged hot or cold. Cold forging these metals causes them to "work harden." When most metals are hammered or worked they loose their ability to bend and become brittle. To bring them back to a soft condition they can be annealed. Bring them to dull cherry red heat and immerse in water. This eliminates the effects of work hardening.

Hot-forging of copper and brasses is easier than working them cold. Naval bronze, phosphorus bronze and silicon bronze are good materials for hot forging. The small percentage of tin gives it a good forging quality, but not the full working range of iron. Lead is an alloy in some brass and causes it to crumble when heated in the fire. It also contaminates the fire and air with lead.

Monel can be forged hot and is best worked around the higher range of temperatures, from a bright red up to a light orange. Monel is an alloy of nickel and copper (400 series, 60 Ni, 40 Cu) and has a great high temperature strength. It also has a great sensitivity to sulfur which causes it to crack or show check marks on the surface of the metal. Because of traces of sulfur in coal, it is better to use a gas furnace when forging monel.

Dry Ash Stick Test for Temperatures of Metals

A test for lower temperatures encountered when forging aluminum and brass is to rub a dry ash stick on the hot metal. The temperatures are indicated by the effects on the stick. This test is also useful when heating iron in the blue heat range.

660°F.	Becomes sticky
680°F.	More greasy
700°F.	Starts to slide
720°F.	Slips easily and starts to smoke
735°F.	Sips very easily, smoke and a few sparks
750°F.	More sparks
770°F.	Lots of sparks
790°F.	Starts to flame

Aluminum can be forged hot or cold. To anneal it, bring it up to a heat that causes a pine wood stick to burn when sliding it over the metal. This is also the temperature at which it can be forged hot. The melting point of aluminum is around 1200°F. When heating aluminum, it will not show you an incandescent color like iron, just a puddled blob of melted metal.

Type of Steel	Series Designation
Carbon steels	XXX
Plain carbon	10XX
Free machining, resulfurized (screw stock)	11XX
Free machining, resulfurized, rephosphorized	12XX
Manganese steels	13XX
High-manganese carburizing steels	15XX
Nickel steels	2XXX
5.00 percent nickel	25XX
Nickel-chromium steels	3XXX
1.25 percent nickel-0.06 percent chromium	31XX
1.75 percent nickel-1.00 percent chromium	32XX
3.50 percent nickel-1.50 percent chromium	33XX
Corrosion and heat-resisting steels	30XXX
Molybdenum steels	4XXX
Carbon-molybdenum	40XX
Chromium-molybdenum	41XX
Chromium-nickel-molybdenum	43XX
Nickel-molybdenum	46XX and 48XX
Chromium steels	5XXX
Low chromium	51XX
Medium chromium	52XXX
Corrosion and heat resisting	51XXX
Chromium-vanadium steels	6XXX
Chromium 1.0 percent	61XX
Nickel-chromium-molybdenum	86XX and 87XX
Manganese-silicon	92XX
Nickel-chromium-molybdenum	93XX
Manganese-nickel-chromium-molybdenum	94XX
Nickel-chromium-molybdenum	97XX
Nickel-chromium-molybdenum	98XX

Chart 19. S.A.E. specification numbers.

Videos

Moran, W. F., Jr. *The Making of a Knife.* American Bladesmith Society, PO Box 977, Peralta, NM 87042.

O'Neill, P. Lambrecht, J. Terry, J. and Meil, P. *Samuel Yellin's Legacy: The Story of a Metalworking Shop* and *The Tree of Iron.* Documentary Educational Resources, Watertown, MA 02172   617-926-0491

Check ABANA listing for video rental and purchase.

Points Carbon	Properties	Uses
5-10	Soft, plastic	Rivets, repoussé, stampings
10-20	Tough	General forging, case hardening
20-30	Quite tough	Structural, machine parts
30-40	Really tough	Crane hooks, machine parts
40-50	Great toughness, little hardness	Axles, gears, shafts
50-60	Great toughness, some hardness	Crowbars, garden tools
60-70	Toughest, fair hardness	Fullers, flatters, forging dies
70-80	Great toughness, hard	Hammers, rivet sets, wood chisels
80-90	Quite Tough, hard with fair edge	Cold chisel, hammer dies, springs
90-100	Tough, hard with medium edge	Knives, punches, taps, reamers
100-110	Little toughness, really hard	Drifts, swages, stone drills
110-120	Great hardness with keen edge	Planing tools, wood working tools
120+	Extremely hard, brittle	Razors, glass cutters, engravers

Chart 20. Carbon steel and uses.

Type	Group	Quench Medium	Wear Resistance	Toughness	Hardening Depth	Relative Cost	Resistance to Decarburization
L	Low alloy	o, w	med.	med.-high	med.	low	high
F	Carbon-tungsten	b, w	low to high	low-high	shallow	low	high
P	Mold steel	a, o, w	low to high	high	shallow	med.	high
W	Water hardening	b, w	fair to good	good	shallow	lowest	highest
S	Shock resisting	o, w	fair	best	medium	med.-high	low-med.
A	Cold work	a	good	fair	deep	med.	med.-high
D	Cold work	a, o	best	poor	deep	med.-high	med.
O	Oil hardening	o	good	fair	med.	low	high
T	Tungsten based	o, a, s	very high	low	deep	highest	low-high
M	Molybdenum	o, a, s	very high	low	deep	high	low-med.
H	Hot-work:						
	Cr based	a, o	fair	good	deep	high	med.
	W based	a, o	fair-good	good	deep	high	med.
	Mo based	a, o, s	high	med.	deep	high	low-med.

Chart 21. Comparative properties of tool steels.

The Flypress   By Brad Silberberg

The flypress, or hand-operated screw press is a versatile and powerful machine that can be used for hot or cold straightening, bending, forming and chiseling of metal. The press is not a substitute for a power hammer or treadle hammer, but can be used to achieve some of the same results as these machines.

1. Frame Configuration. "C" frame presses are more versatile because there is less frame in the way and long work can be "side loaded" into the press. "U" frame presses are stronger because the frame supports the screw on two sides.
2. Screw specifications. The greater the diameter of the screw, the stronger the press. Press screws usually range from about 1-1/4" to 2-1/2".
3. The Cross Arm. The longer the cross arm, the greater the mechanical advantage. Some larger presses have a wheel instead of a cross arm.
4. Weights. There must be some kind of weight on the cross arm for the press to do anything but the lightest work. The greater the weight, the more tonnage the press will generate.
5. Press Bed. The bed of the press should have some means of fastening bottom tools to it. Tee slots are great for bolting down work. Most presses have at least two threaded holes in the bed.
6. Table. Most presses have either a fitted cast iron table or legs that bolt onto the bed.
7. Depth Stop. A stop enables you to get the same ram travel every time. This is very important when chiseling or making production run parts.
8. Cross Arm Orientation Adjustment. The cross arm should be able to be lifted from the screw and re-attached in another position of rotation.
9. Handles. The best handles have an end that will turn on their long axis, saving your hands from blisters. One handle is enough on a small press. A big press should have two, so that two operators can slam it home.

Carbon and Low Steels	
L2 to L7	Low Alloy
F1 to F3	Carbon-tungsten
P2 to P21	Plastic-mold
W1 to W7	Water Hardening
Cold Work	
A1 to A10	Medium Carbon, Air Hardening
D1 to D7	High Carbon, High Chromium
O1 to O7	Oil Hardening
Shock Resisting	
S1 to S7	Shock Resisting
High Speed	
T1 to T15	Tungsten Base
M1 to M47	Molybdenum
Hot Work	
H10 to H19	Chromium
H20 to H39	Tungsten
H40 to H59	Molybdenum

Chart 22. Tool steel types.

Action of File on the Metal	Approx. Rockwell C	Temper Color	Temperature
Scratches glass	65+	Not Tempered	
File slides off part	60	Pale Yellow	400°F
File will hardly mark	59		420°F
File just marks	58		
File marks		Straw Yellow	450°F
File hardly catches	57		
File marks deeper		Deep Straw	500°F
File scratches deeply	55	Light Purple	530°F
		Dark Purple	550°F
Files with difficulty		Blue	570°F
Files begins to cut	53	Light Blue	600°F
File cuts easily	50	Steel Grey	660°F

Chart 23. File test.

Metal	#/Inch³	Melting Point °F	Melting Point °C
Aluminum	.0924	1220	660
Aluminum Alloys		890 to 1215	
Babbitt		480	
Cast Iron	.261	2060 to 2210	
Chromium			1890
Copper	.317	1970	1083
Copper Alloys	.296 to .319	1650 to 1750	
Gold (24K)	.697	1945	1063
Iron (pure)		2795	1535
Steel (1020)	.282	2680	
Lead	.407	620	327
Lead Alloys		150 to 630	
Monel		2480	
Nickel			1453
Nickel Alloys		2440 to 2950	
Silver (Sterling)	.38	1640	961
Stainless Steels	.28 to .29	2500 to 2790	
Tin		450	232
Tin Alloys		280 to 1170	
Tungsten			3410
Wrought Iron	.267 to .285	2700 to 2900	
Zinc	.248	785	419

Chart 24. Melting temperatures and weights.

Guage #	BWG Birmingham or Stubbs	Lbs. per Sq. Ft.
4/0	.454	
3/0	.425	
2/0	.380	
1/0	.340	
1	.300	
2	.284	
3	.259	
4	.238	9.375
5	.220	8.750
6	.203	8.125
7	.180	7.500
8	.165	6.875
9	.148	6.250
10	.134	5.625
11	.120	5.000
12	.109	4.375
13	.095	3.750
14	.083	3.125
15	.072	2.812
16	.065	2.500
17	.058	2.250
18	.049	2.000
19	.042	1.750
20	.035	1.500
21	.032	1.375
22	.028	1.250
23	.025	1.125
24	.022	1.000
25	.020	0.875
26	.018	0.750
27	.016	0.688
28	.014	0.625
29	.013	0.562
30	.012	0.500

Chart 25. Gauge numbers and weights of sheet steel.

Pipe Size	O.D. in Inches	Schedule 40, Standard			Schedule 80, Extra Heavy		
		I.D.	Wall	# / ft.	I.D.	Wall	# / ft.
1/8	.405	.269	.068	.244	.215	.095	.314
1/4	.540	.364	.088	.424	.302	.119	.535
3/8	.675	.493	.091	.567	.423	.126	.738
1/2	.840	.622	.109	.850	.546	.147	1.090
3/4	1.050	.824	.113	1.130	.742	.154	1.470
1	1.315	1.049	.133	1.049	.957	.179	2.170
1 1/4	1.660	1.380	.140	1.380	1.278	.191	3.000
1 1/2	1.900	1.610	.145	1.610	1.500	.200	3.630
2	2.375	2.067	.154	2.067	1.939	.218	5.020
2 1/2	2.875	2.469	.203	2.469	2.323	.276	7.660
3	3.500	3.068	.216	3.068	2.900	.300	10.250
3 1/2	4.000	3.548	.226	3.548	3.364	318	12.500
4	4.500	4.026	.237	4.026	3.826	.337	12.500
5	5.563	5.047	.258	5.047	4.813	.375	20.780
6	6.625	6.065	.280	6.065	5.761	.432	28.570
8	8.625	7.981	.322	7.981	7.625	.500	43.390
10	10.750	10.020	.365	10.020	9.750	.500	54.740
12	12.750	12.000	.375	12.000	11.750	.500	65.420

Chart 26. Pipe sizes and specifications.

Pipe Forging

Pipe comes in two basic forms: pipe made from sheet that is rolled to desired diameter and seam welded, and pipe that is extruded from a solid piece. The seam welded pipe is readily available in many sizes and inexpensive, but forging it can split the welds at times. The solid pipe is more expensive but does not split when forging and can be used in structural applications.

Pipe forging offers the blacksmith different forging opportunities and some unique techniques. Many of the same basic forging processes can be used. For drawing and bending it is sometimes necessary to fill the pipe with dry silica sand and cap the ends. Peter Happny has developed a number of techniques with pipe. Several are: upsetting the pipe and allowing the end to fold and ripple; welding a solid in the pipe and the solid can then be treated in the normal manner and folding and crimping thin walled pipe. Experiment with square tubing by folding, nicking and twisting.

Schools

There are many good blacksmithing and metalworking schools holding classes. Most of these schools offer different types of classes during the year. It is best to contact them for the schedule to check on the type of class you would like. These classes range from beginning to advanced and are taught by leading national and international blacksmiths.

Arrowmont School of Arts & Crafts
PO Box 567
Gatlinburg, TN 37738   615-436-5860

John C. Campbell Folk School
Brasstown, NC 28902   800-365-5724
A program that covers a wide range of smithing activities; taught by leading smiths. Twelve fully equipped work stations.

Colorado Rocky Mountain School   Francis Whitaker
1493 County Road 106
Carbondale, CO 81623   303-963-2562
A wide range of classes and workshops lead by Francis "Dean of American Blacksmiths" and other professional smiths; covers the basics to advanced smithing.

Connecticut School of Wrought Iron Design   Walter Scadden
Box 8116 Buckland Station
Manchester, CT 06040   203-646-8363
Specializes in architectural iron work in a well-equipped and organized shop.

The Forgery School of Blacksmithing   Robb Gunter
13 Imnaha Road
Tijeras, NM 87059   505-281-8080
A well-equipped shop limited to six, beginning and advanced, students per class. Week long or special week-end classes taught by Robb who covers all the subjects. His specialty is practical metallurgy, gas fired forge furnaces and applications.

Penland School of Crafts
Penland, NC 28765   704-765-2359
An extensive number of classes with a wide number of guest instructors covering all metalworking topics; a well-equipped shop and special focus sessions.

Peters Valley
Layton, NJ 07851   201-948-5200
A full range of workshops, covering traditional to contemporary topics, with 10 work-stations; gas and coal forges along with power hammers. Long weekend or full week classes.

Turley Forge Blacksmithing School   Frank Turley
Rt. 10, Box 88 C
Santa Fe, NM 87501   505-471-8608
A number a classes held through out the year covering beginning to intermediate topics; 12 work-stations.

Major Suppliers

American Galvanizers Association
12200 Iliff Avenue, Suite 204
Aurora, CO 80014-1252

Galvanizing information and resources

800-HOT-SPEC

Art Essentials of New York Ltd.
Three Cross Street
Suffern, NY 10901-4601

Gold leaf supplies and books

800-283-5323

Atlantic Steel Corp.
35-27 36th Street
Astoria, NY 11106

Tool steel
Atlantic 33, non-tempering tool steel
212-729-4800

J. G. Braun Company
7540 McCormick Blvd.
Slokie, IL 60076

Steel, bronze, stainless ornaments and supplies

800-323-4072

Centaur Forge Ltd.
117 North Spring Street
Burlington, WI 53105

Large list of smithing supplies, tools and books
Extensive catalogue
414-763-9175

Carolina Glove Company
PO Box 820
Newton, NC 28658

Kevlar gloves are available in pairs or as lefts only.

800-438-6888

Carpenter Steel Division
Reading, PA 19612

Complete listing tool steels

Crucible
5639 West Genesse St.
PO Box 991, Camillus, NY 13031

Complete listing tool steels

800-365-1185

EZ Products
3204 Preston Highway
Louisville, KY 40213

Brazing supplies and a handy propane torch by
Bernzomatic, the Sure Fire

Bill Gitchner
Iron Age Antiques
Ocean View, DE 19907

Tools, power hammers and books.
Specializes in anvils, books and power hammers
302-539-5344

Goodwin-Cole
8320 Belvedere Ave.
Sacramento, CA 95826

This is where I got my tipi.

916-381-8888

Grainger

Complete catalogue of hand tools, motors and supplies
800-473-3473 ext-1053

Norm Larson
5426 Hwy., 246
Lompoc, CA 93436

Books and more books

805-735-2095

Latrobe Steel Co. Latrobe, PA 15650	Complete listing tool steels 412-537-7711
Lawler Foundry Corporation PO Box 320069 Birmingham, AL 35232	Ornamental metal components and accessories 205-595-0596
Little Giant/Mayer Bros. 420 4th Corso Nebraska City, NE 68410	Replacement parts for Little Giant power hammers 402-873-6603
Little Tree Designs 115 E. Mendocino Ave. Willits, CA 95490	Treadle hammer kits and tools for the blacksmith 707-459-1934
McGill Distribution 605 Holland Road Simpsonville, SC 29681	Henrob Torch which uses less gas and is a small useful oxy-acetylene torch 803-963-9805
NC Tool Company 65 Hunt Road AR Pleasant Garden, NC 27313	Gas forges and tools 800-446-6498
Sculpt Nouveau 625 W. 10th Ave. Escondido, CA	Dyes and finishing kits for metals 800-728-5787
Timpercove Trading Company 121 H Street Petaluma, CA 94920	Peddinghaus blacksmith equipment 707-778-8261
Teledyne Allvac PO Box 5030 Monroe, NC 228110	Complete listing tool steels 800-537-5551
Tennessee Fabricating Company 2025 York Ave. Memphis, TN 38104	Cast iron components and accessories 800-258-4766
Triple-S Chemical Products, Inc. 1413 Mirasol Street Los Angles, CA 90023	Complete line of patina chemicals 213-261-7301
Universal Saw 1737 Sugar Tree Road Warrensvill, NC 28693	A universal saw blade for hacksaws 910-385-3401
C. S. Van Gorden & Son, Inc. 1815 Main Street Bloomer, WI 54724	Gun blueing solution 715-567-2612

Organizations

There are a number of organizations that support blacksmithing and metalworking. Many have regional chapters and an extensive list of members. Most also have publications which report on activities, recent work and tips/techniques on metalwork.

ABANA
Artist Blacksmiths of North America   Janelle Gilbert Franklin
PO Box 1181
Nashville, IN 47448   812-988-6919

The art and craft of blacksmithing has enjoyed a resurgence. This increase in popularity of the art has been fueled in part by the dedication of the Artist-Blacksmiths' Association of North America (ABANA). This non-profit corporation was formed over twenty years ago to help foster and promote artistic blacksmithing by:

- encouraging and facilitating the establishment of training programs for aspiring smiths;
- disseminating information about tools, material and equipment;
- exposing the art and craft of blacksmithing to the public;
- serving as a center of information about blacksmithing to all other interested groups and the general public;
- providing a vehicle for blacksmiths to share techniques that enhance and improve the craft.

ABANA has established itself as the largest blacksmithing organization in the world. Their quarterly magazine, the *Anvil's Ring*, includes articles and pictures featuring the finest ironwork. *The Hammer's Blow* is also published by ABANA and its focus is on the "tips and techniques" aspects. Join the network!

BABA   Richard Quinnell
British Artist Blacksmith Association
Rosebank, Plaxtol
Sevenoaks, Kent
England, UK TN 15 0GL

The British equivalent of ABANA also with a quarterly publication. An excellent way to get an overview of the international scene and what is happening in other countries.

National Ornamental Museum   Jim Wallace
374 West California
Memphis, TN 38106
901-774-6380

The only full time metal museum in the USA with a large collection of all kinds of metal artifacts, books and a slide library of 10,000. They have many special shows and hold workshops and demonstrations in their large well-equipped shop.

NOMMA   Barbara Cook
National Ornamental & Miscellaneous Metals Association
804-10 Main Street, Suite E
Forest Park, GA 30050

A 33-year-old organization devoted to fabrication of decorative and structural metals. Publishes *Fabricator* six times yearly and a newsletter. They hold annual conventions.

Bibliography

This bibliography is limited to some of the more important books about metalwork that I have found. It is a greatly short-ened version from the first *Edge*—this bibliography is meant to stimulate your search. These books form only a partial answer, for as the Chinese sage Lin Yu Tang said, "A wise man reads both books and life itself."

Andrews, Jack. *Samuel Yellin, Metalworkers*. Ocean City, MD: 1992.

Aston, J. and Story, E. *Wrought Iron, Its Manufacture, Characteristics and Applications*. Pittsburgh, PA: A. M. Byers, 1939.

Bealer, Alex W. *The Art of Blacksmithing*. rev. ed. New York, NY: Funk & Wagnalls, 1969.

Bollinger, J. W. *Elementary Wrought Iron*. Milwaukee, WI: Bruce, 1930.

Cathcart, W. H. *The Value of Science in the Smithy and Forge*. London: C. Griffin, 1916.

Decorative Ironwork: *Some Aspects of Design and Technique*. London: Council for Small Industries in Rural Areas, 1962.

Edwards, Ifor. *Davies Brothers Gatesmiths*. Cardiff, Wales: Welsh Arts Council, 1977.

Ffoulkes, Charles. *Decorative Ironwork, from XIth to the XVIIth Century*. London: Methuren, 1913.

Gardner, J. Starkie. *English Ironwork of the XVII and XVIII Centuries*. London: B. T. Batsford, 1911.

Geerlings, Gerald K. *Wrought Iron in Architecture*. 2nd ed. New York, NY: Bonanza, 1957.

Handbook. 8th ed., *Forging and Casting*, vol. 5. Cleveland, OH: American Society for Metals, 1970.

Hanks, K and Belliston, L. *Draw, A Visual Approach to Thinking, Learning and Communicating*, Kaufmann, 1977

Hasluck, Paul N. *Smith's Work*. London: Cassell & Co., 1899.

Hughes, R. and Rowe, M. *The Colouring, Bronzing and Patination of Metals*. London: Thames and Hudson, 1991.

Ilgen, William L. *Forge Work*. New York, NY: American Book, 1912.

Kauffman, Henry J. *Early American Ironware, Cast and Wrought*. Rutland, VT: Tuttle, 1966.

Johnson, Carl G. *Forging Practice*. Chicago, IL: American Technical Society, 1940.

Lillico, John W. *Blacksmith's Manual Illustrated*. London: Technical Press, 1930.

Richardson, M. T. *Practical Blacksmithing*. 4 vols. New York, NY: M. T. Richardson, 1891.

Schumacher, E. F. *Small Is Beautiful*. New York, NY: Harper Colophon, 1973.

Schwarzkopf, Ernst. *Plain and Ornamental Forging*. New York, NY: John Wiley, 1930.

Simmons, M. and Turley, F. *Southwestern Colonial Ironwork*. Santa Fe, NM: Museum of New Mexico Press, 1980.

Sonn, Albert H. *Early American Wrought Iron*. 3 vols. New York, NY: Charles Scribner's Sons, 1928.

Smith. H. R. Bradley. *Blacksmith and Farriers Tools at the Shelburne Museum*. Shelburne, VT: Shelburne Museum, 1966.

Smith, Cyril S. *A History of Metallography*. Chicago, IL: University of Chicago, 1960.

Palmer, F., Luerssen, G. and Pendleton, J. *Tool Steel Simplified*. 4th ed. Radnor, PA: Chilton for Carpenter Technology

United States Steel. *The Making, Shaping and Treating of Steel*. 7th ed. Pittsburgh, PA: United States Steel, 1957.

Weygers, Alexander. *The Making of Tools*. New York, NY: Van Nostrand, Reinhold, 1973.

Whitaker, Francis. *The Blacksmith's Cookbook*. Vail, CO: Fleming Publications, 1986.

Williamson, Graham Scott. *The American Craftsman*. New York, NY: Crown, 1940.

Internet

A frequently asked question is "What is the Internet?" Bob Rankin in his on-line document, *Accessing the Internet by E-Mail*, gives this definition:

"Internet (noun) - A sprawling collection of computer networks that spans the globe, connecting government, military, educational & commercial institutions, as well as private citizens to a wide range of computer services, resources and information. A set of network conventions and common tools are employed to give the appearance of a single large network, even though the computers that are linked together use many different hardware and software platforms."

An important development of the Internet is the World Wide Web (WWW) which is a graphic interface of the net. It allows for graphics, sound and videos to be broadcast over the net. As difficult is this concept is to understand it is not difficult to use. If you understand how to use a computer it will not be hard to use e-mail or surf the net on the WWW.

Other than communication with e-mail in your decision to get on-line consider how your exposure and sources of information can be enlarged by having access to the WWW. There are also many sites to find fellow artist-blacksmiths, technical information, materials and supplies.

This short introduction to the Internet represents only a peek at the "sprawling collection" of information available—an open door to the future. Presently there are two Web sites that are sponsored by blacksmiths and metalworkers to help open this door; they are:

ArtMetal

http://wuarchive.wustl.edu/edu/arts/metal/
http://www.artmetal.com/

ArtMetal was first established on August 3, 1994 with the official opening of "The ArtMetal Project" at Washington University's wuarchive. Considering that the web was only a couple of months old at that time, you might think of ArtMetal as one of the metalworking pioneers in this new cyberspace frontier. They were the first artistic metalworking site to settle on the web and continue to bring you some of the best information available for the artistic metalworking profession.

Many people have helped with the ArtMetal Project, and ArtMetal continues to work with anyone interested in contributing to the ArtMetal archives at Washington University. But ArtMetal is growing, and they have now expanded their services to the metalworking trade via the artmetal.com site. This new commercial site is bringing greater opportunities to artists and businesses desiring to market their products to the world via the ArtMetal Village and the Internet.

The other thing you may want to do when you get on the Net, is to join in the discussions being held on the ArtMetal mail list by talented metalsmiths from all over the world.

To subscribe to the ArtMetal mail list send an e-mail message to:
listproc@mail.wustl.edu
Put in the body of the message:
subscribe ARTMETAL<your name>

If you are interested in setting up shop in the ArtMetal Village contact them at:
village_info@artmetal.com

Yellin Job Cards

A abbreviated set of the Yellin Job Cards was originally published in *Samuel Yellin, Metalworker.* The complete set of Yellin Job Cards on a HyperCard stack is now available at:
http://wuarchive.wustl.edu/edu/arts/metal/Yellin/job cards.sit
A text version of the job cards is at:
http://wuarchive.wustl.edu/edu/arts/metal/Yellin/job cards.txt

Artist-Blacksmith Association of North America

http://wuarchive.wustl.edu/edu/arts/blacksmithing/ABANA/

The Artist-Blacksmith's Association of North America (ABANA) is a non-profit art and education organization. Their focus is art metalwork, both contemporary and traditional. Galleries of artistic metalwork, educational offerings, excerpts from their publications, chapter news letters and metalworking resources are found at this site.

The Forge is ABANA's E-Mail discussion group which shares questions and information about the art/craft of the Artist-Blacksmith. Sign up by going to their Web site above.

Ordering Books

To order SkipJack books contact BookMasters our fulfillment service via:
1-800-247-6553
Check out the books at the SkipJack web site and read sample chapters at:
http://www.bookmasters.com/skipjack

Comments

I would like to hear your comments about the *New Edge*, contact me at:

Jack Andrews
1408-B Ocean Pines
Berlin, MD 21811 USA   1-410-208-9098

skipjack@shore.intercom.net e-mail

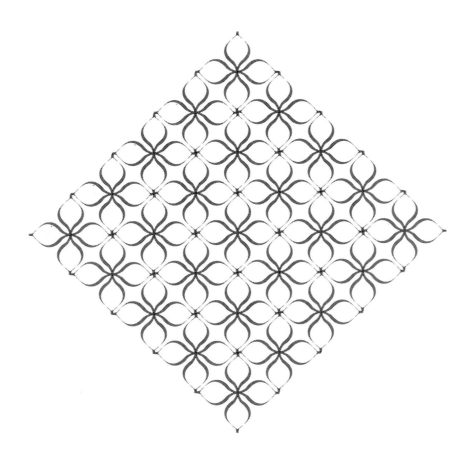

Index